"A BEAUTIFUL COMPILATION ABOUT THE THREE ASPECTS OF LOVE"

#LOVE

A NEW GENERATION OF HOPE

BEST
SELLING
AUTHOR

Compiled By
Anita Sechesky

REGISTERED NURSE, LIFE COACH
LAW OF ATTRACTION & N.L.P. PRACTITIONER

#LOVE

A NEW GENERATION

OF HOPE

Anita Sechesky — Living Without Limitations Publishing
BRAMPTON, CANADA

Anita Sechesky – Living Without Limitations
asechesky@hotmail.ca
ansechesky@gmail.com
www.anitasechesky.com

Publisher's Note: This book is a collection of personal experiences written at the discretion of each contributor.

Book Layout ©2014 Anita Sechesky – Living Without Limitations

#Love – A New Generation of Hope
Anita Sechesky – Living Without Limitations.
ISBN 978-0692317921
ASIN 0692317929

Book Cover: Steve Sechesky
Inside Layout: Steve Sechesky

TABLE OF CONTENTS

LEGAL DISCLAIMER

The information and content contained within this book *#Love – A New Generation of Hope* does not substitute any form of professional counsel such as a Psychologist, Physician, Life Coach, or Counsellor. The contents and information provided does not constitute professional or legal advice in any way, shape or form.

Any decisions you make and the outcomes thereof are entirely your own doing. Under no circumstances can you hold the Author or "Anita Sechesky – Living Without Limitations" liable for any actions that you take.
You agree not to hold the Author or "Anita Sechesky – Living Without Limitations" liable for any loss or expense incurred by you, as a result of materials, advice, coaching or mentoring offered within.
The information offered in this book is intended to be general information with respect to general life issues. Information is offered in good faith; however you are under no obligation to use this information.

Nothing contained in this book shall be considered legal, financial, or actuarial advice.

The author assumes no liability or responsibility to actual events or stories being portrayed.

It may introduce what a Life Coach, Counsellor or Therapist may discuss with you at any given time during scheduled sessions. The advice contained herein is not meant to replace the Professional roles of a physician or any of these professions.

FOREWORD

CHARLOTTE HOWARD

Every year in November, I begin to prepare for my New Year's resolution by asking myself how I can improve. I pray to God for his continued guidance and support as we all know He is in control. One of the top things I wanted to accomplish in 2014 was to make a big difference in the lives of others.

I truly believe that God puts people together for a reason to make a bigger impact in the world. When I met Anita, I was going through a tough time in my life, just like many of you who are reading *#Love – A New Generation of Hope*. Anita understood that I was having a rough time and she was there for me as a sister, business partner, and a friend.

People are going through challenges in their lives every day. Some people have self-esteem issues, self-confidence issues, anxiety, mental and physical abuse, just to name a few. How many of you have reached out to them as a friend to see how you could support them? Love for yourself and others are extremely important in life.

Whatever you hand out to the world, you'll get back. Basically, it's the Golden Rule - do unto other people what you'd like other people to do unto you. Try it for yourself. The next time you're out and about, smile at somebody and say "Thanks." 99% of the time, you'll get a smile back, as well as a generous "You're welcome." That's a really simple example.

What you hand out to the world should be considered a gift. What should we accomplish with this gift? Mother Teresa said, "Give your hands to serve and your hearts to love." Anita didn't know this but I truly felt the love she provided to me just by the way she asked me how she could help when I was dealing with things. I am often asked by clients how they can create an abundant life. I believe the first step to creating an abundant life is by having love for yourself, others, and sharing love simply for the greater good.

Abundance really begins with you – inside you, not outside yourself. You send it out into the universe. In that way, you're increasing your own inner abundance by sharing it with other people. It will be sent back to you when you least expect it. As you practice this, you'll find you've opened a window, letting in astonishing possibilities for yourself and other people. The more you share, the bigger your world will be, with more alternatives than you've ever dreamed possibly existed.

A different component of abundance, possibly the most crucial component, is a sense of gratitude which is also shared in *#Love – A New Generation of Hope*. Without gratitude for what you get, you'll wind up blocking yourself again from the natural flow of abundance. There's power in the universe; one that demonstrates the give and take of that natural flow. Your brain and heart need to be in harmony with that power to really enjoy abundance in your life story.

Gratitude is essential to keep your mind aligned with the thought that the supply of abundance is limitless. It's really simple to slip into the mentality of scarcity instead of abundance; so try to prevent it from happening. The minute you feel yourself moving back into the abundance mentality, say thanks out loud for all that you've got and all that you're yet to get.

It's a great idea to sit down and write out all the blessings you're thankful for in your life. If you're feeling down, it's a particularly great time to remind yourself of all you have, rather than perpetually thinking of all you feel you don't have. I'm a big believer in "gratitude journals" and recording daily all that I'm thankful for in my life.

If your household is cleared of the clutter, then you are able to bring in what fuels your soul, delights your brain, and thrills your heart. Bring in the meaningful things, the genuinely beautiful pieces.

It's crucial that you decide what you wish in your life, according to your own personal values, and then arrive at a decision to take action involving those values. By simply adding love, you invite abundance into your life story. As long as your household and your brain are cluttered with stuff, there's no room for the flow of abundance. Simplify your life.

Not only will you start to feel better about yourself, it will begin to show in everything you accomplish. It will show in how you interact with loved ones, friends, and business partners. You'll be more at ease, happier, less stressed, and much relieved in your heart and in your brain.
#Love – A New Generation of Hope will touch your heart and soul.

Charlotte Howard
charlotte@thehairartistassociation.org
www.successinbeauty.net

ACKNOWLEDGEMENTS

It is with great pleasure that I take this time to acknowledge the people who have stood by, supported, and loved me for who I have become today. I am so grateful to God for this blanket of love that continually surrounds me and lifts me up. These individuals have contributed to the woman that I am and it is because of their unconditional love towards me that has inspired and supported my dream to do more for others. Their love has helped me to grow emotionally through my own life experiences so that I can assist others to do the same.

I would like to now take this opportunity to acknowledge Stephen, the love of my life for believing in me and my desire to always strive for greater purpose in all that I do. Your unconditional love and friendship have inspired me in this journey. Thank you for being who you are to me and our boys.

To my eldest son Nathaniel: Thank you for being such an amazing son. I love you more and more each day. You inspire me and make me so proud to be your mother. You are an intelligent, kind, and loving individual. I adore your sense of humor and appreciate all the special gifts God has blessed you with to appreciate knowledge and seek wisdom in all your ways. Always remember what an amazing gift from God you are, to not only your family, but also to those around you. Never give up on your dreams. You were a success from the day you were born. I believe in you. Love Mom.

To Samuel: Thank you, my darling son for the joy that you bring to Mommy. I love your curiosity as a child, always fixing and taking things apart. You have the mind of a genius with so much potential. The world is unfolding before your very eyes. You never cease to amaze me with your growing wisdom and skills. God has great plans for you. Success is in every step that you take. I'm so proud to call you "My darling little boy." I believe in you. Love Mommy.

To my beautiful mother Jean Seergobin: Thank you for always encouraging me to see the beauty in the world around me and encouraging me to never give up, you are my best friend mom and I love you dearly. To my distinguished Father, Jetty Seergobin: Thank you for showing me how to never be discouraged in life but to carry on despite whatever circumstances I may be facing in life. Mom and Dad: I love you both so much, because of your love for me. I have never given up on doing more for the greater good. You each have inspired me to be a better person and look past my own fears, failures and the criticisms of others. I am so blessed to have you as my parents. May God bless us all with long and healthy lives together as a family. I love you Mom and Dad.

To my handsome brother Trevor Seergobin: Thank you for allowing me the room to grow professionally and chase after my dreams, one of them becoming an International

Best Selling Author. Your continued support, encouragement and praise makes me think of you more as my big brother and I'm so proud to call you my brother. I believe in you too!

For all of the people who have been part of my life and supported my dreams and ambitions, thank you for being the wonderful friends, colleagues and family that you are too me. I love and appreciate each and every one of you for who you are.

Once again I would like to give an unusual appreciation to those who have caused me heartache, disappointments and pain. Because of you, I never gave up in life, it was your hardships that you put me through which made me strive harder to believe in unconditional love that is lacking in this world. Two wrongs never make a right. I forgive.

DEDICATION

This book is made possible by the love that has surrounded me in my life. I would like to dedicate this Anthology to my children, Nathaniel and Samuel, and all the children represented around the world.

You are all the hope of a new generation of love.

Anita Sechesky

INTRODUCTION

My intention for all my books is to help bring a global shift of hope and healing. But for this specific anthology project, *#Love – A New Generation of Hope,* I decided to switch it up and create a topic based on what I highly regard as one of the most important things in this life.

I believe Love is so powerful that it can bring healing and hope to those who need to be accepted and cherished. Love can heal relationships because of the sensitivity involved when you are connected to another person. Love can help you make choices that are life-changing. Love can give someone the strength to survive through the worst of circumstances in their life. Love can bring enemies together and create a peace that was never there. Love is unspoken but yet powerful enough to create a shift so great it can unite two completely opposite people.

I have based this anthology on three specific themes which I have characterized as the three aspects of love and are identifiable by everyone. I strongly believe that we are always exposed to at least two, if not all three, of these aspects. This book was birthed from my vision of helping to create awareness that love is the one thing we as human beings have in common. It is the invisible thread that can join nations and change the world if we only can see how powerful it really is.

My purpose of this book is to help others learn and gain insight on how viewing these three perspectives can positively affect one's life. I decided to break down what love really is on an observational level and how it relates to the relationships in our lives. I believe that each of these themes is an integral part of every person. We are wonderfully and beautifully made specimens of humanity. We carry emotional attachments to the people, places, and things that we experience on a personal level. The very act of living and existing in this world itself is a powerful medium which allows us to form valuable and intimate relationships with many individuals. For a large majority of our human population, the norm is to be born into a family network where we are cared for and nurtured with love, affection, and training to grow up as successful individuals who develop into mature and confident members of society.

This beautiful book was remarkably constructed from the heart strings of each one of my contributors who decided they wanted to be part of something bigger. During our initial consultation, each co-author felt compelled to share a personal story from their heart with the purpose of bringing more love into a world that is in great need of it today. These stories and memories are real and they will reach your very core. It doesn't matter who you are or where you come from. Your life is one that needs love to survive as a healthy and well-rounded individual and more than likely you have already given this love back to those around you. So many people live with a lack of gratitude for the lives they have and unfortunately carry baggage that is weighing down their hopes and dreams in life. Maybe you have been so heartbroken or discouraged that you believe your life does not have the same value or importance as others. You can release all those broken and lonely emotions that continually attract negativity and a life of bitterness and gloom. How amazing for you if you have learned to love yourself again after being let down by life events, whether it is physical, mental, emotional, or things that may have attempted to destroy you altogether. You are a very unique and blessed individual if you chose not to let what you struggled and walked through become your roadblock in life.

The stories in this book are aligned with the vision that God placed into my heart at a very young age. I knew what it felt like to be the outcast and the one who didn't fit in. I was the one who had the different skin color than others my age because my family had just emigrated from tropical South America to North-western Ontario when I was just a young child at the sweet age of four. My once playful and carefree life was instantly transformed from living in a hot tropical country where I had already been introduced into the Nursery School system with great friends that loved and played with me. I was accepted! It was the place I remember that when it rained tropical buckets there were huge mud puddles to jump in afterwards. Obviously this was much to my mom's dismay as she had me all dolled up in my white socks and sandals with my perfect little dress full of ruffles and trim. Such is life when you have parents who were a tailor and a seamstress, and had their own business. I guess you can say it was like being a little princess even though my family was not well off at the time. Interestingly enough, years later when I was a teenager, I recall hearing my parents discuss how my dad the tailor was offered a contract with a very prestigious airline to design the flight attendants' uniforms. Imagine if we had stayed! I really would have been that little princess in all sense of the word. However, my parents decided that having the opportunity to raise their family in Canada would be a better choice at the time. It was a decision that was not made lightly and it was never looked back upon.

We relocated to North-western Ontario and I had to learn a whole new way of adapting into a society that was in the deep freeze in the middle of winter with temperatures falling to minus forty. Yes, it was a very brutal cultural shock for all of us. Not only was the climate cold, we soon discovered the citizens in this part of the world were not the warmest at times either.

So you see my book *#Love – A New Generation of Hope* is something that has always been a part of who I was as a person. I grew up and became trained as a Registered Nurse working in various hospital departments to now specializing as an Emergency Room nurse and have cared for many people. I learned about tolerance at an early and young age. However, it took a good part of my life to understand that a huge part of acceptance towards others involves searching your own heart to understand that individuals respond to situations and other people based on how they are feeling within their own hearts and souls.

Many of these stories are written from perspectives that are quite amazing when you really begin to understand that each person we encounter is in a journey of discovering who they are in the bigger picture of life. I requested my writers to choose a specific theme they felt was the most insightful approach they could share to the world about the love that is constant and the love that releases who they are into those around them. I asked them to search within their souls and bare their inner emotions about where they once were and compare it to where they are today in their journey.

As the main author, visionary, and also the publisher of this book, it brings me great joy to present these true life inspiring and beautiful stories of hope, healing, inspiration, and of course love. It always amazes me how the human spirit is so strong and resilient to endure experiences that we as humans may face at any given time in our lives but are not always brave enough to talk about.

For me personally my faith, as well as the love and knowledge that someone belonged to me and I belonged to them, is what brought me through many adversities. Our lives are so connected and many times people do not realize that the reason they are struggling in their lives is due to love being absent – whether it is from a parent, child, spouse, relative or friend. Yes, love is the energy that connects all of these relationships. It is a positive, healing, and concealing power that covers up our mistakes, carries our pains and disappointments, makes us feel welcome and secure, and still does so much more. For those of you who are lacking love in their lives, cannot fill the void, and often times seek fulfillment in the wrong places, please know you are loved, you belong, and you are valuable because someone else needs you to love them back as well.

Don't ignore or neglect the love that is in your life. Love is a powerful energy that can change your whole world: one thought, one action, and one kind gesture at time. #LOVE.

LOVE
FOR
SELF

ANITA SECHESKY

Anita is a Registered Nurse, Certified Life Coach, International Best Selling Author x 3, Speaker, Trainer, Publisher, NLP and LOA Wealth Practitioner, as well as Big Vision Consultant. She is the CEO and Owner of Anita Sechesky - Living Without Limitations. Anita has assisted many people break through their own limiting beliefs in life and business. She has two International Best Sellers and is launching her first solo book *"Absolutely YOU! –Overcome False Limitations and Reach Your Full Potential"* in November 2014. As a professional compiler and publisher, Anita can help you to put your passion on paper.

www.anitasechesky.com
asechesky@hotmail.ca

ONE

....

LOVE FOR SELF
FROM A HEART OF GRATITUDE

In order for an individual to acquire a true nature of love for self – from a heart of gratitude, there must be a divine connection to your source, whatever you may perceive that to be. We all come from somewhere outside of who we are in our physical state of being. For some people, this means a divine connection to the Creator of the universe. Ultimately, we must understand that our lives are intricately fashioned in such a way that for us to continually evolve into our greatest self, we must fearlessly journey within our hearts and souls to discover the secret passion that will propel us into well-being and bliss. It is not an easy journey as many will admit because as human beings, we are our worst critics and many times the limitations and perceptions that we hold on to are based upon the most unique, perplexing experiences, or labels that were placed on us during times of vulnerability and life events.

As creatures of habit and reaction, we based our life's journeys on the things that we are comfortable with, many times staying within our comfort zone, refusing to step outside the box or take a chance on what may come. In doing so, we are in a stagnated growth emotionally and mentally, all the while physically progressing. We continue to age and develop as our appearance changes, our behaviors are second nature, and our choices have become predictable to those close to us. In order for there to be real growth and evolution, we must choose or allow new and thought-provoking experiences to challenge our very core. You see, sometimes stagnation is misinterpreted for peaceful tranquility and sometimes peaceful tranquility is misconstrued as bliss. When an individual testifies to reaching the ultimate awareness of inner peace and harmony, magnified by the power of love and contentment, they are very well describing the state of bliss. This is the oneness with your environment and everything within your soul. It's up to you to determine where your life is taking you in your journey along this path of evolution. As we experience more setbacks, failures, challenges, highs and lows in life, relationship roller coasters, and mental stimulation through advance training and skills, life will test us to change our reactions and predictabilities. The choice is ours.

For many this means that they have entered into a space of sacred understanding and in order to co-exist in a world of so much distortion, corruption, and negativity, one must be able to understand the center where their heart is at peace. It may be through a connection to God or the universe, which is something much bigger than us. This space will have to be where there is an abundance of peace and love. Speaking from a heart of appreciation, you must be able to control things which you may never have done before. For someone to achieve this state of gratitude, they must understand that life is a story that they get to co-create. Our thoughts create our reality, based on our emotional attachment to the outcome. People often equate miracles and positive outcomes to the understanding that they have deposited a measure of faith, good thoughts, and positive affirmations towards their generated outcome. Many times, life's harsh experiences are the contributing factors causing people to demand within themselves that which makes them invincible. Life's past events have established a foundation of strength and tolerance, enabling individuals to be empowered so that they won't just tolerate any more setbacks, but instead choose a life that responds to the joyful nature of having stillness and not mindlessly reacting as they may have before.

Along life's journey, the human spirit perseveres through many trials, tribulations, and triumphs. As we are tested in many directions, we develop a template of our personalities. The following stories throughout this book touch on things of this nature. For instance, developing and seeking a life of gratitude can begin in childhood based on both negative and positive events. It will impact the very essence of that person who experiences these situations to seek out and question, challenge, and change past, present, and future events. These may include not fitting in, having to face life threatening conditions, an unexpected pregnancy, abusive relationships, family break-downs, as well as a variety of other reasons. Remember, many times what happens may not be directly related to who you are, but life will give you many experiences related to the vibrational energy of those you are closely associated with. You just may happen to be a recipient from the spill over of those you have interacted with at any given point. That being said, as we enter into self-development and transformation modes, we as responsible beings come to recognize and appreciate the greatness that is within us and how magnificent a gift it really is to rediscover what we have lost through our journey. Suddenly, we are adults facing our own situations and relationships, careers, and opportunities from a whole new point of view. This time, it's all about us and how we are managing our lives. In doing so we are forced to make decisions all over again. It's your life and you get to choose despite what you have already walked through.

How often in your life do you actually take time out to appreciate all that you have around you, whether it is close and loving relationships, friends, or families? What about being grateful for what you have survived and endured?

People do not realize that each and every relationship in their lives are a profound and intricate network of the many facets and roles they have to support in who they are as individuals. It doesn't have anything to do with whether they are negative or positive, the very fact that you are connected with others is a confirmation that you exist. In order to be recognized and appreciated, you must be validated which means that you have a personality, an opinion of how you perceive life, and how you choose to show up in the world. By understanding that your life has equal value, just as those you are connected with, allows your higher self to appreciate and connect with others on a more authentic and sincere level. This is a huge deal for those who have suffered from neglect or abusive and traumatic experiences where they were vulnerable enough to allow the situation to scar them. Although this may have happened unexpectedly, it DOES not mean it was the victim's fault in any way, shape, or form. It just means that the awareness of the pain has actually strengthened the individual enough to shift them from a victim mentality to self-empowerment.

A heart of gratitude is cultivated from such profound and often times life-altering experiences. A familiar saying states that people will continue doing the same thing over and over, expecting a different result each time. Unfortunately, they don't recognize that the key solution is introducing a whole new perspective that opens windows of possibilities, allowing room to breathe and grow. I often wonder about how it would impact the lives of those who seem to be stuck in a difficult and lonely state if they would only choose to be open-minded enough to appreciate that in order to love the life they have been blessed with, they must develop a continual process of forgiveness and love in their lives. Releasing the baggage and heartache resulting from the unforgiveness and pain of others, as well as themselves, will allow the trapped negative energy and low vibrations to be changed. As they choose to make an effort of forgiveness and gratitude in their thought processes, verbal responses, emotional triggers, and behavioral reactions, it will bring positive and higher vibrational energy that the power of love is comprised of. This change of attitude will continue attracting more of the same positive experiences and it will feel like a huge weight has been lifted off.

For anyone to gain a life of blessings and bliss, one would have to choose to be loved and appreciate everything that has ever happened to them as they cannot change the past, but can create a future of happiness, peace, and love. It may take a whole journey revisiting and finding strength in the journey. I will be honest – from my own experiences, if there are unresolved events in one's life, there will be some sort of stagnation and blockage of blessings. But a whole new renewal of perspectives can create a major shift in future outlooks and outcomes.

Love for oneself from a heart of gratitude is one of the most gratifying journeys you can enter into. May your travels be blessed.

If You Care About You...

If you care about you...this is what I would do. I would look at what the world has to offer and then look at what my world is lacking.

My world is made of many things. They may be small to you, or they may seem strange from a different point of view.

I'm not sure where you are coming from, or what encompasses your world.

I would add all the things that make me smile, even if it is for just a little while. I would make a note to not forget the memories that have etched a mark in my heart!

If you care about you...this is what I would do!

Anita Sechesky

Love Me As I Am – As I Love You Just As You Are.
I will be the first to admit that I am not perfect. I cannot deny that I have made mistakes. I know there are many things about myself that can be improved, and trust me, I am working on them...one day at a time.

I know that not everyone will like what I like. I also know not everyone will like me. I am thankful for everyone I have had the pleasure to meet in my life. Many I had the honor of knowing for so long. I am thankful for everyone and am looking forward to the future and to many I have yet to meet.

I appreciate every opportunity that life has given me to make special moments when I can.

I feel empathy for those who think just because they have something more than me, have done something I haven't, are older, more well known, or established – because of their mind blocks that they have created in their own world, they cannot learn something from me and my life experiences and journey thus far.

I welcome every opportunity to grow, yet still stay young! I embrace every challenge that has come to me as a lesson to be learned somehow at the turning point. My simple advice to you is to live life fully so you never miss the blessing to become a better you!

Sometimes our journey is filled with much company and sometimes not. Love yourself in such a way that you can still appreciate the humanity in others as you see yourself...just as vulnerable.

Anita Sechesky

Journey

Not everyone will resonate with what you are saying at any given time. Each one of us has a different journey in life to make. Our gifts and contribution to humanity may not all be the same. But somewhere deep within lies a secret of your greatest fears.

Think of precious moments — the ones fleeting and in disguise; the ones that lasted but a second and yet remain in demise. Learning to let go of all your fears is not a religious act or feat. Accepting that we all face these obstacles makes more sense and easier a defeat! Once you have conquered all your inner foes, you can then begin to walk delightfully into all we like to call your flow. Not many will understand what I am really saying; not many will care to know. But those who catch a drift of this indeed will have a far, far way to go!

Anita Sechesky

Life Is Too Short!

Life is too short to be concerned about the people who don't care. There will always be someone bigger, better, stronger, braver, smarter, prettier, and richer!

Life is too short to be concerned about the people who don't care. There will always be someone who is jealous of thee.

There will always be someone who doesn't care about you or me!!

Why worry, fret, or cry? They never really cared and it really doesn't matter why!

Life is too short to be concerned about people who don't care.

Move on and do your best. Let your dreams unfold and it will take care of the rest!

You are one in million and one is all it takes to make a difference in your life!

Anita Sechesky

W. A. READ KNOX

Read is an International Best Selling Author and Certified Life Coach living in Hunt Valley, Maryland, USA. He is the father of five children and has one grandchild.

Read is a Realtor and has experience in numerous businesses over the years involving Aviation, Trucking, Mortgage Banking, Natural Health, Professional Sports, Frozen Foods, and licensed Life and Health Insurance and Investment Broker. Read is an avid athlete with a passion for Squash, Tennis, Skiing, Motorcycling, Polo, Hockey, Sailing and Travel. Interested in ReDox Science and its ability to change our health through Bio supplementation.

knoxread@gmail.com
facebook.com/read.knox

TWO

···

F.L.Y.

FIRST LOVE YOURSELF

On Thursday, October 13th, 1983 I made a decision to leave my entire life behind for thirty days to enter rehab to recover from alcohol and drug abuse. At the time, I had a good job working for a bank. I had a beautiful wife and an amazing little girl. My wife was expecting another child and I was not able to quit drinking on my own. I was stopping by the liquor store on my way home from work every night and buying a few small bottles of vodka to make healthy fresh squeezed orange juice or grapefruit juice infused with vodka – again and again – followed by some wine. I didn't have a problem drinking because I did it every night, and I didn't feel well at all the next day until I got home from work and had a drink – which usually turned into several. On that Thursday, I made the resolution to get off the roller coaster and I asked for help by calling the employee assistance program hotline at work. "Sure you can have a glass of wine with dinner up there," the counselor lied to me. "Just be there tonight with your bag packed and we will take care of everything else."

Rehab was an amazing experience where I learned a lot about myself as well as my fellow in-patients. Every family has problems and most alcoholics and drug addicts have to deal with chronic severe circumstances created by their addictions. I had my eyes and heart opened during the following thirty days of rehab. When I attended my first support group meeting which was later the next night, I felt amazing that I had finally met my people. I sensed that I belonged and was amazed to hear story after story of how the effects of alcohol had created an abundance of problems for so many people. I was not in the wrong place after all and as the days passed I came out of a fog that I didn't even know I was in at the time. I was one of the lucky people who go to a rehab and stay sober by the grace of God, my own efforts, and the power of the treatment program, one day at a time. To this day, I have been blessed with over thirty years of clean and sober living.

Sobriety alone will not solve all problems and my life has had many of them, but I have never had to take a drink and have endured some pretty harsh experiences as well as some pretty awesome ones that could be celebrated easily with many drinks. The ups and downs of life are the times when the cunning, baffling, and powerful Alcohol is at its best. Over the years I have seen many people relapse when they have been at the heights of accomplishment. More frequently the depths of despair take their toll on an alcoholic/drug addict, and depression and mental illness of one kind or another is revealed. The importance of Love in overcoming these formidable obstacles cannot be under estimated.

Firstly, the addict/alcoholic must love him/herself in order to really enjoy living sober. This was the greatest gift that I received while in Rehab. After much introspection I discovered that I carried a lot of rage, guilt, and shame inside and I chose to forgive myself for all of the things that I had done in the past. This was a process that didn't happen overnight and is a continuing practice that helps to keep me sober one day at a time. I forgive and love myself every day. I use positive affirmations and thoughts to feed my mind, and healthy alkaline ionized water, fresh organic fruits, vegetables, and meat to feed my body. I am slowly becoming a vegetarian as much as I am able. I am learning new things about health every day and applying this knowledge to my life.

Because my body is made of trillions of cells and each of these are amazing little bags of salt water that have DNA, mitochondria manufacturing the glutathione and other key antioxidants and proteins that keep my body healthy, it is imperative that I use the power of my conscious and subconscious mind to love myself. How I think and what I think can affect my body and my life, and I must be ever vigilant of this reality.

Six years ago I underwent a very serious heart operation where I had an aortic root and valve replacement due to a congenital bicuspid aortic valve and aneurysm that had grown to a dangerous size. My heart was damaged in the surgery and I now am 100% pacemaker dependent. I am very lucky to be alive and feel grateful to have recovered from this surgery which was the most difficult thing I have been through in my life. I wrote about this experience in a chapter of the International Best Seller "*Living Without Limitations – 30 Stories to Heal Your World*", also compiled by Anita Sechesky.

Recently I was diagnosed with bladder cancer. I had just finished playing a vigorous game of doubles squash and used the restroom prior to taking a shower. I filled the toilet with a great deal of blood in my urine and immediately had memories of my father's battle with bladder cancer. I called an urologist, was seen within 48 hours, and underwent a CT scan with contrast and a number of other tests that confirmed the cancer diagnosis. I was once again filled with apprehension and fear about what choices I would have to make regarding a treatment plan. I had watched my father die from bladder cancer after a long battle that had also started by urinating blood. His treatment was a major surgery which simultaneously removed his bladder, prostrate, urethra, and appendix after which his urine was collected in a bag for the rest of his life. He lived for five more years after the surgery but during a follow up checkup it was discovered that the cancer had spread to his liver. There were numerous small spots of cancer visible in the MRI scans that were spread throughout the organ. The doctors advised that there were several chemotherapy drugs they could try but the likelihood of survival was not good. After trying about four different drugs, none of which had any positive effect on the cancer, my father eventually starved to death. I feel that the chemotherapy contributed greatly to his cause of death, however there were few if any alternatives offered by the doctors. There were no databases fifteen years ago to go to in order to help make a decision as to which potential therapy may give the most likely positive outcome.

So I went on the internet and researched bladder cancer and had the good fortune to meet a woman whose husband had just been diagnosed a year ago and had been recommended the same treatment my father had undergone. They refused this treatment plan and sought out natural methods of healing his cancer. They radically changed his diet and began juicing fresh vegetables and cut out white flour and all sugar. They took up a vigorous daily routine of meditation, strict diet and vitamin supplementation, and exercise. They rebuilt and strengthened his immune system with all natural means and today he is cancer free. What an amazing miracle of LOVE this is. This woman loves her husband so much that she healed his cancer all naturally. She has just finished writing a book about their experience and I highly recommend it to anyone touched by cancer.

I underwent a cystoscopy surgery in my bladder and had all of the visible cancer removed by my urologist. I am so lucky that I had the symptoms of my cancer early enough to have caught it before it made it through the wall of my bladder. I will be checked every three to six months for any recurrence of the growth of cancer in my bladder. Bladder cancer tends to recur as often as 80 percent of the time so I also have taken on a new regimen of having fresh pressed organic juices and supplements daily. I have also continued to exercise and eat as organic and as vegetarian as possible. I am educating myself about all of the newest findings of quantum science and medicine and the role of redox signaling molecules in cellular health and regeneration. All diseases are cellular and we are learning more everyday about how what we eat, what we think, how we emote, and how we live our lives affects our cells and our health.
Love plays a huge role in our health.

DARLA OUELLETTE

Darla is an accomplished Registered Nurse with over ten years' experience in various disciplines. She also holds two other diplomas, one for Registered Practical Nursing and Law and Security Administration. Darla's love for writing and creativity began at an early age in high school. She wrote poems in Literary Books at school, and at home, daily. Darla has chosen to combine her love of writing, nursing career, and life story in this compilation.

Darla was born and raised in Wallaceburg, Ontario. She is the third child of four children in her family, and was raised by her mother on her own. She too is a single mother of a wonderful teenage son, Cameron.

DarlaJO88@gmail.com
DarlaOuellette@hotmail.com

THREE

....

THE JOURNEY WITHIN

How has this happened? I've worked so hard for everything I have, and given so much. Negative $366.54, that's what my bank account balance was. I sat there, devastated and in shock. I began to cry, and wonder how I would make it through this difficult time in my life. A single mother without an income and an injured back. Away from my family and longtime friends.

It all started back home in my small town of Wallaceburg, Ontario. There were very few jobs and none as a Registered Nurse. I had worked so hard to get my Nursing License. I worked through a failed marriage, supported myself and my son on OSAP, and started off on a new journey as a Registered Nurse. I was excited about all the new possibilities that were awaiting me. I had passion, a zest for life, and dreams of a new life for myself and my son. Not being able to find a job in my hometown was just a setback, but why not venture out and see what other cities had to offer? This is where my journey began, working in London, Ontario as an R.N. I had been working at the hospital for 3 years on a busy Medical and Respirology Floor. Things were going well. The job was stressful but I was learning a lot and making a decent income. I had decided to move my son and myself to London. The driving back and forth was taking a toll on me and I didn't like being away from my son for so long. It was approximately one hour and a half drive from my home town. So we made the move to a much bigger city and found ourselves overwhelmed but managing with all the changes. My son was sent to a babysitter while I worked.

All seemed to be going well until that one midnight shift, April 18, 2009. I had injured my back repositioning a patient. I thought of course at first that I just sprained my back and would need some rest. Unfortunately, it turned out to be much worse. I struggled daily with the pain, but had little time off work. My doctor at the time didn't think it was anything serious. I decided I should get back to work and everything would be fine. Time passed and the pain never went away, it became impossible to do certain tasks at work and home. Bending, lifting, and twisting of my lower back was unbearable. I was given permanent restrictions through Occupational Health and my Doctor. Then, the current floor I was working on became no longer safe for me. The hospital decided to transfer me to the Neonatal Intensive Care. There would be little to no lifting with the little babies. I was again excited to venture out into a new field of nursing. Learning new skills and expanding my knowledge was always thrilling to me. So I began training in this new unit, scared and a little overwhelmed but eager to learn. Unfortunately I had only been in the unit for a short time when my back pain again became unbearable, unmanageable, and overwhelming.

I saw an orthopedic surgeon in early 2011. He agreed that the Neonatal unit I had just transferred to was not suitable for someone with my condition and ordered an MRI. After it had been reviewed, everything began to change. After years of suffering, they had determined what the real problem was, and that it would affect me forever. I would have chronic pain, and it wouldn't heal. Surgery was not an option. The surgeon said I should go to the Chronic Pain Clinic and suggested I receive Facet Injections. I had the facet Injections, three in total, with little to no relief. I saw Chiropractors, Physiotherapists, Massage Therapists, Reiki, Acupuncture, and even started taking natural anti-inflammatory medications. I took several different types of pain medications, tried ointments and rubs, ice, heat, and regular exercise. I had my last day of work in April 2012 and remained off, unable to cope with the pain. I had run through my sick leave pay at work. I had ran through short term disability, and wasn't qualified for long term disability because I wasn't "disabled" enough. I sunk into a deep depression. Lost weight and cried almost daily. I lost all energy and hope of having a normal life. How could I cope with such horrible pain every day? Nothing seemed to work. Everything made me tired or gave me other adverse side effects. I started seeing a Cognitive Behavior therapist. It did help, but on a limited income I could no longer afford to go. Funds were running out and fast! I felt so lost and didn't know which way to turn. I began to lose all hope of ever being happy and began to have a very poor self-image.

One day, my neighbor dragged me out to walk our dogs twice a day. I started to feel a little better physically and less stressed. It was the first time in years that I had been allowed to give my body the rest it needed. I began traveling back home to see my old chiropractor, and visit family and friends.

All this time I had no word from work and no resolutions. I felt frustrated with the system and angry that I was forced to go on Employment Insurance and then eventually Social Assistance because WSIB had denied any further claim and my sick leave from work was long gone. The hospital representatives, my union, and I met in January of 2013 to discuss possible accommodations. I felt there was maybe some hope at getting them to accommodate me in another position. Still, nothing happened. Now, I had no income and was faced with tough decisions once again. I decided to move back to my home that I had been renting out while in London. I would be closer to my family, my friends, and hopefully move past all this disappointment and despair. Still, I felt alone. I felt like a failure. I felt like I was moving backwards. After all, hadn't I moved to London to create a better life for my son and myself? I couldn't help but think, "Why had this happened to me? Why was I sitting here with negative $366.54 in my bank account? What would I do for money? How would I survive?" That's when things began to change for me. It didn't happen overnight. It didn't happen instantaneously, or because of some miracle, although I do believe in them. I began to pray and regain my faith in the Lord. I began to listen for the answers to my prayers, for some guidance in the right direction. I began to believe that things could get better. I began to learn to appreciate things and be grateful for all the things in my life, no matter how small. I began to make a shift in my perspective. I began to believe I could reclaim the happiness, love, peace and joy that I wanted by making some of these changes. If we can learn to have gratitude, we can move forward from the dark places we find ourselves in. We can achieve greatness......

Lesson 1:

Be grateful for EVERYTHING you have in life. It is a gift. The air you breathe. The food you eat. The sleep you get. Your friends. Your job. Your family. Waking up for a new day to begin. If you start to learn to appreciate the little things in life, you WILL start to feel a shift to a more positive outlook on life. Gratitude is very powerful and can help heal your soul from many ailments.

Lesson 2:

Have faith in the Lord. He created us and gave his life for us. He is the way to happiness and a loving life. He does listen and answer your prayers. He puts forth a lesson in life for a reason and it's up to us how we choose to respond and deal with that lesson. He often places two paths before us and we choose the direction we take. Speak to him often and ask him for guidance as to which direction to take. He will answer your prayers and make the direction clear to you.

Lesson 3:

Be kind and loving to yourself. You are responsible for you. We must take care of ourselves before we can even attempt to care of others. We must learn to give ourselves the rest, sleep, time, love, and patience that everyone deserves. We must listen to our bodies and give them what they need. We need to rejuvenate our minds, bodies, and souls often. Even take a few moments a day to catch a few deep breathes and reconnect with yourself.

Lesson 4:
Don't get caught up in the rough parts of the journey along the way. Everyone has difficulties and struggles within their lives. We have all lost and felt hurt, felt sad and overwhelmed. We cannot let ourselves get caught up in the negativity of it all. This is all part of our life lesson. Life is a lesson, and a journey. It is not meant to be hurtful or knock you down. The bad things or rough patches in life happen for a reason. These lessons placed before us are to make us aware that we are off course and need to point ourselves in a new and different direction. A good friend once told me, "Rest if you must but don't stop! Always get back up and move forward." Anything is possible.

Lesson 5:
Accept the bad things, the tragedies, losses, and hard times in your life. It is okay to allow yourself to feel anger, despair, disappointment, and heartache. It's okay to shed tears and have your time to let it all out. We are human. We have emotions and it's healthy to express them. The key is to not let it consume you! This is the important part: Let it go! Once you have forgiven that person, experienced anger about a situation, shed tears of sadness, and grieved, you must move forward by telling yourself this moment has passed. I don't like what has happened but what can I do to change it? I love the Serenity Prayer because it's so powerful and true.

Lesson 6:
Allow only a select few people into your inner circle. This doesn't mean to not let people into your heart and your life. However, your most personal thoughts, feelings, values, morals, and ideas are valuable. You don't have to tell the

world about your problems and issues. There are unfortunately people out there that will sometimes use this knowledge and turn it against you. There are people who are negative and pessimistic. They are demanding of your time and like to try and bring other people down to their level of despair. These people are often not bad individuals but rather those who are searching for that self-love, that happiness, that faith, gratitude, and that positive shift in their lives. So keep a small close circle of good friends that are supportive, trustworthy, faithful, positive, and uplifting in your life.

I hope these lessons have helped to inspire you to make a positive shift and change in your life. These lessons have helped me turn my life around. They have helped me find my inner strength, my love of self again, and true happiness. Every day is a different day and we have challenges placed before us. However, if we have a positive attitude, are grateful for what we have, have faith, and love ourselves unconditionally, we can achieve anything and make a shift towards a more positive and fulfilling life!

JANEL SIMPSON

Janel is a respected Youth Leader, Counselor, Mentor, Advocate, Educator and a Visionary – whose purpose is to transform lives through her Ministry. Over the last 10 years Janel has mentored and counseled various youth and families going through difficult times.

Janel is the Founder of Emmanuel Life Management Center whose vision is to see young people liberated socially, academically, and spiritually to take on their God given purpose to serve their families and communities.

Janel Currently resides in Brampton, Ontario and is an extraordinary mother and role model to her son. She holds a Bachelor's Degree in Sociology and a diploma in Law & Security Administration.

www.elmcgroup.org
simpson0590@gmail.com

FOUR

....

GOD CHANGED MY HEART
180 DEGREES

I overcame my pain and hurt with a strong mind and willingness to forgive and love again. The series of traumatic life experiences I have been through at an early age was enough to cause me to forget about loving or even caring a bit about anyone else. Most notably, I was shot with a gun by "mistaken identity" and having to live with that horrible feeling was terrorizing. The worst part was not being able to talk about it with anyone. I felt people would believe it's some kind of T.V. show or even a bad dream if I chose to share with them. However, the truth is that it was my reality.

Not only was I overly sensitive about this topic but my scars were a constant reminder of what had occurred that night. They were visible enough to cause people to ask questions. Sometimes when I was asked about my scars, especially on my back or my shoulder, I would lie simply because I was afraid of opening up that particular chapter of my life. I would then feel guilty afterwards but it was less painful than explaining my story all over again. I used to be very conscious of people judging me, considering in Canada, handguns are usually associated with "wrong doing or bad people." Each time I remembered that night when those men tried to take my life I would relapse on how I felt about people, especially young men that hung out at the malls, wearing hoodies or baggy clothing. I became skeptical of young people and their imaginations, wondering how the hell they thought and reasoned in their minds. I was constantly questioning how much people really loved and cared for each other. Thinking about a group of men foolishly wanting to take my innocent life at such a prime age made me angry. Yes, I was bitter!

The day I understood God's love was the day I began walking in total freedom. I realized I had to let go and let GOD. This physical, mental, and emotional frustration was bigger than what I could have fought alone. The "let go" I speak of means releasing me to love and forgive. I never imagined I would trust again. During my university years, going through the physical and mental healing process, I was more interested in senior students. The thought of a group of younger persons together usually creeped me out. I was judgmental towards young people in general, strongly perceiving the idea that they could be delinquent at any given time without a cause. Unfortunately I even misjudged other positive and respectable adolescents as a result of not trusting anyone. I began segregating myself from those whom I felt were not either educated or enrolled in a college or university. There is the familiar quote "Great minds think alike" and I wanted to surround myself with people that I believe thought the same way as I did.

There were several battles going on through my mind. Separating myself from everyone around me was one of my get away solutions. There were days when I wanted to go missing and become unknown. I imagined sometimes what a pleasure it would be if no one knew who I was or even cared about my story. My circle of friends became smaller and smaller as I trusted less people. Those who read in the newspaper about my shooting incident were fortunate to have heard of my story because I was afraid of discussing it with anyone. This was a precautionary measure because I had a hard time trusting whom to tell. If I was not careful someone, or even the assailant, could come back and retaliate. The shooter was "unknown" to police, therefore the question remained: who could it be? There were people I knew that had no clue about what happened to me and I decided to keep it that way.

Trusting was my major challenge. However, with God's grace I gave myself permission to trust. I told myself it was okay to forgive. Forgive those young men. Forgive that situation. I forgave myself for holding on for so long. I became very interested in God all over again. I wanted to understanding mankind. I sought to learn more of God's love. I began praying and reading my bible more. When I came to this spiritual understanding, I finally found freedom and peace. I couldn't help but notice that a lot of things were changing around me. My energy was more positive. I was no longer playing the blame game. I grew stronger and less concerned with what people felt or thought about my situation. People's opinion wasn't relevant at this point in my life. I noticed God had given me a renewed mind and a transformed heart. A heart that was flesh and not stone. A heart that was ready to give love, embrace love, and love again. I was longing for that liberty and wanted to experience this newfound heart.

Growing up, I have been through and witnessed enough traumatic and depressing situations that would qualify me as a lunatic. On the other hand, I've realized that it was not God's will in my life to go through these tests without a testimony. He has purposed me to do great things in this world. I always felt that one day I would build up the strength and courage to open my mouth and expose those evil and violent people in this world. Sometimes I ask myself "Who really cares?" I remember those days that all I could feel was bitterness. I resented people that carried guns and I wished they would all die. Often time I was frustrated, especially when I heard of other gun violence amongst young people and innocent children. During my early recovery stage, I felt that young men were "potential killers." This is indeed an over generalized statement but when you feel hope has left the building, peace no longer exists, and love is still unborn there was not much to look forward to. I felt as if a generation of potential, purposeful, and passionate young people has been revealed as failures. I could not see any hope for the next generation. I even thought of my children and their children as I wondered about the kind of world we lived in. Young people shooting other young people like birds in the woods. This was my reality and it was scary imagining this behavior becoming an accepted norm in society. Gun violence and people senselessly killing other people was once upon a time a news broadcast or an interesting western movie. Never did I dream of this becoming my story.

I always hoped to get over these feelings one day and use it as a learning tool. Looking back and being reminded of how strong I am, how brave I am, how I overcame, and how much God loves me would be my proof of becoming a winner. Thank God I became tired of complaining. I was sick of watching other young people destroying themselves. I became sick of hearing the problems being addressed without any real solutions. I wanted to make that difference and to use my hurt to show the world that good can come out of evil. I wanted to prove to myself and believe that God could use my pain and hurt to heal others and speak to me. I was able to let go of a hardened heart by the grace of God. I began looking to God for help and strength. A major part of my mental and spiritual recovery was conditioning my mind to operate in God's love and forgiveness. This was indeed a divine intervention where my mind and heart began working together in unity. I was more compassionate towards young people and realized they themselves needed love. I felt the need to love people more; to understand them and their behaviors. My heart wept as I now began to see the need for helping and giving back to people especially teenagers.

Today my passion lies in helping those in need particularly young people and families. My positive recovery is now my biggest ammunition to fight against negativity, doubt, fear, and shame. I have made a commitment to give back and help people academically, socially, mentally, and spiritually to become who God has created them to be. I had a vision to operate a charity for youth and address major concerns affecting teenagers and young adults. In 2012, Emmanuel Life Management Center was founded with the hope of transforming the lives of youth. Situations that are affecting teenagers have now become my burden to bear. Through my test and trials I can confidently say I am equipped for this work. Listening has become one of my strongest senses. Sometimes all that people need is an attentive ear, a non-judgmental mind, and a loving heart to embrace.

After I discovered God's love, the desire to give and help became second nature. I almost felt compelled to start a new awareness with absolutely no unanswered question. I found that the biggest confusion in my life was not having any answer to problems I was faced with. Sometimes we ask the right questions but to the wrong person. The wrong people can give us wrong answers that take us nowhere. The Holy Spirit of God came into my life and caused my heart to change 180 degrees. Today I feel love and it brings me joy when I'm able to positively impact someone's life. I can move forward without any resentment, hatred, or anger. My story has become my testimony and I no longer focus on negative things. I am able to identify every young person's need and what they are going through. God has given me a new heart and a ministry. It's very important for me to transform lives, create opportunities, and change young people's negative perceptions on life.

Life is beautiful and should not be taken for granted. We only live once and death is for certain. Harboring hatred and animosity within our being takes away from our lives. We cheat ourselves from the freedom, peace, and happiness that God promised us. It's okay to tell someone, especially a stranger, that you love him or her. Love is kindness and as human beings we were created to love each other. I discovered two major components in life that will make and not break you, strengthen you, and bless you: Love and Forgiveness. Love is a force of nature. However much we may want to, we cannot command, demand, or take away love any more than we can command the moon, the stars, and the rain to come and go according to our whims. A wise idea is to be yourself, flow in that warm spirit, and watch people flock to you. Love is bigger than you are. You can invite love, but you cannot dictate how, when, and where love expresses itself. You can choose to surrender to love, or not, but in the end love can be unpredictable and irrefutable. You can even find yourself loving people you don't like at all. Love does not come with conditions, stipulations, agendas, or codes. Like the sun, love radiates independently of our fears and desires. Love is inherently free for everyone. It cannot be bought, sold, or traded. You cannot make someone love you nor can you prevent it for any amount of money. Love cannot be imprisoned nor can it be legislated. Love is not a substance, not a commodity, nor even a marketable power source. Love has no territory and no borders. Love is of God and God is love!

CATHY HANSEN

Cathy is the newest and only Mobile Mortgage Specialist for a major bank in Thunder Bay, Ontario and the surrounding area. Her smile and outgoing personality along with over 15 years' experience in the financial industry, made her the obvious winner for this new role with the bank. Starting a new life on her own, and a new career, all at the same time may seem like a lot to take on, but with a new energy and spark back in her eyes, she is ready for anything!

cfalzetta@tbaytel.net
facebook.com/cathy.hansen

FIVE

....

WAKE UP!

Have you had a moment where something so obvious drove you crazy because you didn't see it sooner? Almost like the light bulb was on a dimmer switch and then suddenly a power surge goes through every vein in your body! That's what happened to me just before Christmas of 2013. I felt a rush of energy sweep over me which shocked every brain cell forcing me to "WAKE UP!"

My story begins the summer of 1993. It was the last summer I spent with my dad. He passed away that September after a long hard fight with cancer. My dad was my rock who always kept me grounded and was my anchor through every storm. His quiet, patient way of looking at things was always just good common sense. He never graduated high school, but he was one of the wisest people you could ever meet. He wasn't book smart, but people smart. That's the biggest gift he could ever give me. I've got that quality thanks to my dad. Losing him was like losing a part of my body. There was an empty space; a gap so large I thought it would swallow me whole. I didn't know what to do with myself.

Leading up to my dad's final days, I had been living in southern Ontario. I had gone to college there and worked for a number of years. Things were not going great for me in the big cities. I was working in the service industry for crappy wages and my first true, grown up romantic relationship had left me in a pile of debt. I was working two jobs to make ends meet. When I wasn't working at the bank I was doing a shift in a restaurant. Ultimately, this crazy lifestyle caught up to me and I ended up with mono. My health, along with my dad dealing with chemo back home was enough for me to throw in the towel. I headed back north to live with my parents.

My dad lived for a couple of years after I migrated back to Terrace Bay. As much as I hated my job in the local pulp mill, I would never trade one minute I got to spend with my dad for a better or easier job. The last summer was so hard to watch him wither away experiencing so much pain. The day inevitably came that he took his last breath with us holding his hand in the hospital room. They say time heals all pain. That is a downright lie! I don't feel the pain every day like it just happened, but it hurts just as hard every time I think of it. I just don't think of it as often.

My plan wasn't to stay in Terrace Bay. I started applying for jobs in the nearby city of Thunder Bay, but the next chapter of my life happened only months after losing my dad. That was the day I was asked out on a date with the person I would spend nearly 20 years with. Looking back at that day now, I realize that he and his children became the soil that filled in that huge gaping hole in my heart. The vacant space that had once belonged to my best friend and hero was filling in. It took four people and a dog to fill it, but with all the stress of a ready-made family in a short amount of time, I didn't have the time or energy to mourn for my dad! I jumped in with both feet first not having any prior experience. On my wedding day I married four people, not just one.

The honeymoon was over before it started. A month after our wedding, my role changed from part time to full time parent. We were used to having the kids five days out of seven, but after moving we suddenly had them full time. I was tired and continually sore, and we had no social life to speak of. It turned into a survival mode for me. I went to professional counselors many times over these years to find help. I received therapy, read books, talked to relatives, and even went on medication for depression and anxiety. Nothing made me feel better. I gave up my job at the plant so the kids would have someone home all the time. I didn't want them to be juggled around by different babysitters and I couldn't physically perform my job any longer. My decision didn't help the home situation at all. I think it actually made it worse because I felt like I was making all these sacrifices and nobody appreciated them. I felt like I did everything wrong. There wasn't a moment when everyone in our home was happy at the same time. Someone or something would set off a screaming match almost on a daily basis. My inner voice was telling me I was a failure. I felt like I had made the wrong choice to be a part of this ready-made family. But I had made a vow and I truly cared for all of them. I didn't want to let anyone down. My doctor was slow to realize how bad my health actually was becoming, but he finally diagnosed me with Fibromyalgia. I had 90% of the common factors of "Fibro" patients.

The next chapter in my life is when the miracle happened. I found out I was pregnant. My pregnancy couldn't have been easier. I actually had very little pain and felt healthier than I had in years. I went into labor on the anniversary of my dad's death, and my daughter was born the next morning. It was the same full moon, hospital, and nursing staff as the night my dad passed. I know he was there that night when she came into this world. I could feel it! She became my main focus and the days I spent at home with her were the happiest days of my life. Over that course of time, my stepdaughters went to live with their mother, and we moved to a small community just outside of Thunder Bay. After the plant in my home town shut down, my husband got a job with a large hydro company. I was able to go to work part time at a nearby credit union. The peaceful life in the country was good, but I was still in pain on a daily basis and depression was making me a very hard person to live with. I wanted to be more active, but the lack of energy and pain made it almost impossible. I felt as though I had been through a war but I didn't want to fight any more. All I could do was to get through each day. Most times, I would have to take a nap in the middle of the day. The worse my condition got, the more frustrated my husband would become and the stress made it worse. It was a vicious cycle that I was trapped in. It felt like I was drowning. Then things ultimately came to a head one night, as though a volcano that had smoldered for many years finally exploded. The things that were said to me out of anger, resentment, and frustration will stay with me for the rest of my life. I actually wish I had been beaten that night because those wounds would have healed by now. My self-esteem was already low and my inner voices were echoed by this man who was supposed to honor me through sickness and health. It made me take a long hard look at my relationship, or at least what was left of it. After many weeks and hours of talking, I decided to give this marriage another chance. Days, weeks, and months went by, but much changed between us. We were set in our dysfunctional ways.

Seven months after that fateful night I heard a voice. Not my inner voice like you might assume. It was the voice of that first true grown up love relationship that I had had twenty-five years ago. It was the person I had thought I would spend the rest of my life with. With the sound of that voice, a surge of energy went through me like a lightning bolt! I was a puddle of tears from joy, or sadness, or maybe relief. I'm not too sure, but I had feelings that I hadn't felt for a very long time. For the next few weeks and after many late night conversations, I knew that I did not love my husband the way that a wife should love her husband. I still had feelings for this other man. Before I could start another year miserable and unhappy, and making someone else's life the same way, I told my husband I wanted a divorce. We couldn't go on any longer the way we were. Surprisingly he agreed with me. He was actually visibly relieved. He actually complimented me that I had the balls to do what he couldn't do! It reinforced my decision when I realized it was as much over for him as it was for me. I felt empowered that I was taking back control of my own life, and my own happiness. Possibilities of my future were racing through my head. I couldn't wait to start this new adventure! It wasn't completely without doubt though. I had days where I was so scared I had made the wrong decision that I was going to tell my husband to forget the whole thing and take me back, but I didn't. Since I was going to be on my own, I realized more changes had to happen and I started looking for a different type of career. I ended up deciding to take a position as a Mobile Mortgage Specialist with an established company. It's a straight commission sales job that allows me to work from home and be the captain of my own monetary ship.

I finally reunited with my long lost love through social media and soon understood that he was one of those people that come into your life to teach you a lesson. I realized that returning to my past was no way to move forward with my life. I consider him my soul mate and do not regret seeking him out the way that I did. It was his voice that said, "Wake Up! You deserve to be happy. Stop existing and start living!" It made me begin talking nicer to myself, dreaming of a fresh start, and imagining what I was going to do with the rest of my life. I learned that another person cannot make you happy; you have to love yourself first. I don't have my dad to make me feel like I'm special any more, and I don't need any one to do that for me either. I'm an awesome, fun loving, caring person with so much to offer to this world. I still have pain in my life almost daily, but living on my own terms and being the master of my daily choices, I feel as though a weight has been lifted off my shoulders. I hope that one day my daughter will look at me and say that I taught her not to settle for just being in a comfort zone but to take chances in order to live a fulfilling life. I don't know what tomorrow will bring but I'm ready for whatever the world has in store for me. Bring it on!!

JENNIFER MAZUR LYALL

Jennifer is wholeheartedly committed to creating a sacred place where you can connect with your soul, sense your highest potential and embrace your truth & passion fully. She is a Truth Detector, Intuitive Coach, Soul Worker, and Founder of Your Soul Connection. Through energy work, intuitive guidance and her unique modality, Your Soul Connection, she guides you to tune in to your soul, your internal "Truth Detector," and create a solid foundation for you to live a life with intention.

Clients who work with Jennifer develop their intuitive skills, learn how to easily make decisions, and be in a state of passionate awesomeness and flow.

www.yoursoulconnection.ca
facebook.com/yoursoulconnection

S I X

....

C H O O S E   L O V E

A huge part of my spiritual awakening began when I discovered automatic writing in the spring of 2011. It is a form of channeling divine messages. It feels so good as I write the words, the messages, and the insight I have discovered over the years. The messages were always so simple, yet so profound.

Each morning I would rise, early before everyone else in my family, and begin my morning routine. I would meditate, move my body, and write. I would write and write pages upon pages. Some mornings, I would begin with recounting my previous day and how I was feeling or my dreams. Other mornings, I would let myself get into a relaxed and heightened state of being (still in a little bit of a sleepy slumber) and just let the words flow on the paper.

I would receive channeled messages from what I believe to be God, angels, and Mother Earth. Sometimes it felt like I was channeling messages directly from my soul, and other times it felt like messages from loved ones who had passed away years ago. Overall, the messages were positive and encouraged me to be my true self – light and love.

At the beginning, I felt like the messages were so simplistic. I was continuously urged to be love. Oh sure, be love. It's easy eh? Yet, as a mother of two young busy boys, my patience was often tested. How can I do this when there is so much chaos surrounding me? Yet day after day the messages came out, poetically sometimes, sharing the same message over and over. "All of your love is waiting for you. You just need to embrace it with your whole heart. Then you can also begin to love yourself unconditionally." "As you find the missing links, the inner emotional turmoil will disappear...forever."

This sounds so simple; too simple. I found it hard to let go of my old ways all together, however I did notice a gentle softening of who I was being. Although it was still easy to get caught up in the drama of life, I found more and more moments of loving life.

In September of 2011 I wrote:
"Choosing Love: Choosing Love will always serve you. Choosing Love will always support your goals. Choosing Love will always reign in the truth and save you from disaster. Choosing Love will always help you succeed. Choose Love. Be Love."

Ah...those words tasted sweet like candy. Then I would get caught up in the tangles of life again, and lose track of where I wanted to be and who I wanted to be. Yet, there were always the gentle words showing up in my morning musings again to get me back on course.

My morning messages on October 21, 2011 included:
"Being love:
To be love is to be beauty in motion.
To be love is to live life with simplicity, and beauty.

To be love is to be your true self."

"Choosing Love:
   When you choose love, it is like choosing to breathe, choosing to drink, choosing something that is essential to nourishing your body, and soul.
   You need to love to survive. Without a belief in love, a belief in yourself, you will remain stuck in lessons that will be presented over, and over until you see the opportunity to love yourself, and your life.
   To choose love is to choose to live with beauty, acceptance, and with limitless possibilities."

How can you feel anything but love with those words flowing through you? Then the teaching expanded to illustrate how my loving way of being can impact other souls in the universe.

On October 29, 2011, I received these inspirations:
   "Your thoughts and emotions reverberate through the universe, and transform the lives around you.
   The more you are love, the more love and support that will come to you.
   Even in the most difficult times, find the courage to choose love. Love will never let you down. It will set you free."

"True Love:
   People talk about true love and they think about romantic love. The "reality" is that true love goes far beyond that. True love spans lifetimes and universes.
   True love is a state of being, not a state of loving.
   Be true love and bless your lifetime with the ultimate beauty."

Wow – to consider that my love, me simply loving my life could impact others in such a profound way was humbling. I was beginning to witness how my love impacted others in the world around me. When I was gentle and loving to myself, and being love, I noticed other people's mood's also softening. I noticed how the world seemed brighter and the energy that surrounded me was gentler. Problems didn't seem to be problems. Solutions came to me easily and effortlessly. It also came to others easily when they were in my energy field.

I also began to notice the same inspirations I was receiving were echoed in the words of other spiritual teachers, in modern day to ancient wisdom. These same messages have been divinely passed down to many teachers around the world.

"Loving Life:
  Enjoy the beauty in every moment of every experience. It is the only way to love and get the most out of life."

"Love and family:
  Love and family are easy to associate. Every family has its rifts and challenges which give them opportunities to grow. The key is to be love in spite of those challenges, and to let the lessons of those challenges strengthen the family bonds."

"Reasons to love:
  There are many reasons to love.
  It feels good.
  It spreads positive energy throughout the universe.
  It evolves the human race.
  It cures disease.
  It releases humanity from the power of fear."

There it is again – love impacts the universe. Me being love is a gift to the world and beyond.

"Fear cannot exist with love.
Being love for yourself and others is the key to moving forward.
With loving support, there is nothing to fear."

On Friday, February 23, 2012, I wrote:
"My life's purpose is to serve others by awakening them to their higher spiritual powers. The only way to truly do this is through love.
Love awakens, releases, relieves, and surrenders the attachments to the past. When you live in the present, you live in a place of love. When you love, you are powerful, attractive, like a magnet.
Love breaks down barriers like nothing else. Love wholeheartedly accepts a person as they are welcoming them to be, and not be judged. Welcoming them and allowing them to let down the wall around themselves. The front they have put up can melt away.
Love is the safe haven within, and a gift to project out into the world. You give away your power every time you step away from being love.
To be love is to be humble. There is no ego in love.
To love is to be peace. There is no war in love.
Love goes beyond all boundaries to peacefully release the ties, the tensions, between anything and everything.
Love is your angelic hands reaching to untie the knots of ropes that bind people to the existence they are living and sets them free.
Walk in love.
Walk in grace.
Walk in fearless compassion.
For it will lead you to a beautiful place you have always known but have long forgotten since it seems like an impossibility.
To anchor the world in love right now is to anchor the world in peace, and avoid chaos."

Wow! Every moment that I spend in love reaches far and wide across the world. Everything I do for love is not only for myself or the people that surround me – it contributes to the universe as a whole.

As an Intuitive Energy Practitioner this concept began to sink in on a deeper level. When I first began practicing energy work with myself and others, I became preoccupied with needing to protect myself. Some teachers I learned from talked about dark spirits and of incredible things that happened to them when they were encountering them. It filled me with fear while I was clearing energy of others because I didn't want the "dark" energy lingering around my healing space or coming into me. Then a friend of mine told me that the only protection I needed was love. This goes back to the teachings I was writing about. There is nothing to fear when I'm being love. I began to see these "dark energies" as simply being lower vibration of energy that was hanging around to help a soul work through a teaching or "lesson." As the person was ready to let go of this and assimilate the teaching, the "dark energy" released easily.

I started to look at these energies as blessings. I started to see them as wonderful souls that were so committed to the evolution of that person that I was working with. It would share part of its existence with that individual to help them grow and expand. So, as I was working with these energies, I was playing in the universal planes of existence, uplifting the vibration little by little.

I discovered how this could be done, not only with clients who came to see me or whom I helped remotely by phone or by Skype, I could also send this love to other people who needed my help, both loved ones and strangers through prayers and intention. Whether it was praying for someone who was facing a health crisis, or praying for peace in other areas of the world where there was so much turmoil, my intention and prayers could be of service.

As I heard stories and updates from friends about how their loved ones were turning around in their health, I knew the power of love and prayer to be true. Even a dear friend of mine who was going through a cancer journey told me how often she could feel my love surrounding her. You see, even when we didn't speak for several weeks my thoughts would drift to her, seeing her in perfect radiant health. Imagine my love surrounding her and uplifting her to a wonderful space of peace and comfort. She could sense this in her heart and soul.

The honor of uplifting another person is HUGE. I realize that in my gift of helping another, I am also supporting their journey to being love in the world. This means I'm also serving to support the many souls that they too are impacting. It's this wonderful chain reaction of raising vibrations further and further into the universe.

This realization is a gift in itself. I was beginning to embody the teachings I was receiving. As I started to live it and practice being love, that's when more things began to fall into place and life got easier. It was like the universe was taking care of more and more for me. It helped me to see things from a place of possibility rather than looking at the challenges.

What if that could be possible for you? Consider, just for a moment, that life can be simple – that one of the greatest gifts we can give in the world is love. It is something anyone can give at no cost. We are an unlimited source of love, continuously able to generate more. The more you give love, the more it appears to return to you. The possibility of giving love is open to everyone, and anyone, regardless of race, gender, financial status, or religion.

We all have the ability to be love! We can all be gentle and loving souls. We can all cheer up a stranger with a smile. We can all reach out to a friend new or old with a hug. We can all share wonderful positive words to inspire. We can all touch another soul by looking in to their eyes. Imagine what your life could be like simply by infusing it with more love. Imagine what the world would be like simply by you infusing your life with more love.

This concept of love has expanded my love of life, happiness, and my view on what is possible. Come take a walk on this joyous path- our love really can change the world.

OLIVE WALTERS

Olive is an International Best Selling Author, Motivational Speaker, and Law of Attraction Practitioner. She is the Founder and owner of Trecourt Virtual Services Inc. providing virtual customer service, and sales professionals to Fortune 500 companies. Olive is very passionate about inspiring others to believe in themselves, and their vast potential. She teaches them how to use Law of Attraction, and their intellectual faculties to create abundance, results, and peace in their own lives. Olive currently resides in Brampton, Ontario, Canada and is a mother, grandmother, and lover of life.

IAmOliveWalters@gmail.com
facebook.com/olive.walters.90

SEVEN

....

LOVING YOURSELF

Have you made mistakes that you haven't forgiven yourself for? Have you gone through experiences that you blame yourself for or that have impacted your self-esteem? I think we all have. I know I have. Unfortunately living with guilt, unforgiveness and low self-esteem keeps us from living up to our true potential or being happy and that is no way to live.

You may recall my story about surviving domestic abuse called "My Relationship was Red Flagged!" in the International Best Selling compilation *"Living Without Limitations – 30 Stories to Heal Your World"*. Well, following the attack on my life I blamed myself for putting my family in a dangerous situation even though I wasn't aware of the potential danger at the time. I experienced feelings of guilt for not providing one of the most basic necessities that a parent provides for their children – safety. I had a hard time forgiving myself for that. That event also left my self-esteem in shambles. Not only did I feel worthless, but I concluded that I must be the most undesirable woman on the face of the earth. I wasn't interested in getting dolled up to go out every day. I stopped worrying about how I looked and I had these constant recordings playing in my mind telling myself that I didn't deserve love and might as well forget about happiness.

There came a point however when I had to decide and learn to forgive myself. Not that I blamed myself for the abuse, I'm not saying that at all. I know that I had no control over his actions but at the end of the day, I put myself and my children in harm's way by moving in with him. I had to forgive myself for making that disastrous decision. I realized that walking around feeling guilty and beating myself up mentally, emotionally, and psychologically was extremely damaging. I was basically just punishing myself over and over. It's almost as if I went into partnership with the person who hurt me. It was as if we were on the same relay team. He started the race (the abuse) and then I took the baton and continue the race in the form of replaying the events and feeling guilty and undeserving. The problem was, my leg of the race lasted years. I decided eventually that I didn't want to be on his team any more. It was time to drop the baton of pain. It was time to pick up a new baton, one that would provide healing, confidence, and a positive self-image. And that's what I did. Once I realized and acknowledged that by not forgiving myself I was just punishing myself and continuing what he started, it was a no-brainer that I just had to forgive myself.

I had to accept that I am human and make mistakes. And it is okay to make mistakes as long as you learn from them. One way of knowing that you have learned from your mistakes is by doing a Do-Over. That's where you think about or write out what you would have done differently if you could go back and do it again. That way you know that you not only learned from the past but you know that if you had possessed the knowledge and wisdom that you have now, you would have done things differently. We do the best with what we have at the time. Once I was able to accept this basic truth, I was able to be easier and gentler on myself.

I started talking to myself the way that I would talk to a close friend who may have experienced the same situation. I would have told her not to be so hard on herself, that everyone makes mistakes, and that she is a loving, giving, beautiful woman who deserves love and is loved. I would have told her to learn from the experience and not give up on herself. I would have reminded her that she is a strong woman who had risen above other negative experiences and could no doubt come out of this one as a better stronger version of herself. I told myself all of these things. My self-talk changed from negative guilt-ridden garbage to positive strengthening words.

This process worked gradually and I knew that I had forgiven myself when the memory of what occurred didn't hurt, when it no longer had a negative effect on my emotions. No hurt, anger, frustration, or sadness. That's when I knew that I had truly forgiven myself. It didn't mean that I forgot what happened or that I didn't learn from it or that I shouldn't have to pay the consequences, but it meant that when I thought about what happened I didn't feel the emotional pain and guilt.

The next leg on my journey consisted of changing the meaning that I had attached to that event. Whenever something happens in our lives, especially something negative, we tend to attach a meaning to it. For example, you failed a math test in high school so you decide that it means that you are bad in math. Or you get turned down for a date and you decide that it means that you are undesirable and no one is ever going to love you. Neither one of those conclusions is correct but we think them continuously until one day they become our beliefs. And more often than not we live our lives trying to prove that our beliefs are correct. The meaning that I attached to the attack on my life was that I wasn't good enough or worthy enough to be loved. When I realized that I had control over what I thought and as a result what I believed about the event, it was like a thick dark cloud lifted off me. His actions had no bearing whatsoever on my worth. His actions were just that, his actions. His actions were a result of his issues. Once I wrapped my mind around that awareness, I felt so much lighter. If you are going through something where you are looking at someone else's negative actions or words and using them to draw poor conclusions about yourself, I invite you to rethink those thoughts.

After I forgave myself and changed the meaning that I attached to that event it was time to start loving myself. That was the fun part. It took a while and it is something that is ongoing. I'd like to share some of the methods that I used.

I had always had a hard time acknowledging my accomplishments, I'm more likely to downplay them or see them as nothing special. I remember doing an exercise where I had to write down fifteen things that I accomplished and was proud of. I couldn't even think of five. I'm sure a lot of you go through the same thing. Why are we so much harder on ourselves than we are on others?

Why is it that I can look at another single mother who raised two children on her own, bought her house on her own, worked full time and either attended University part-time or worked part-time trying to get a business off the ground and see a strong, ambitious woman? But then when looking at myself, who accomplished these very things, why do I think "Oh that's no big deal. It's nothing to be proud of. Anyone can do that." Why are we so hard on ourselves? Why was I so hard on myself? I still am to a certain degree. It is something that I am continually working on. That exercise was a real eye opener for me. I started re-evaluating my accomplishments and gradually allowing myself to feel good about them no matter how "small"

Another practice that really helped me was being grateful. I know it sounds cliché but when you take time to be thankful for what you have it actually feels good. I like to start my day off with thinking of what I am grateful for. It always starts with "I'm grateful for this comfy bed, the two blankets covering me, my socks keeping my feet warm..." and it just takes off from there. You can be thankful for anything. It doesn't have to be what you think would be impressive or acceptable to others. Starting your day off with this kind of attitude is beautiful. The positive feelings and emotions are like a gift that you can open anytime you want.

Now that all of those warm fuzzy emotions are flowing, it's always good to aim them at yourself. I'm talking about loving and appreciating yourself. That's something that everyone needs to embrace. We are bombarded daily from day one about what is considered the standard of beauty.

Whether it is from the media, society, our culture, family, or friends we are fed images of beauty that only represent a small section of the population. Growing up I always felt inadequate. Even though I had an athletic figure, could eat whatever I wanted and never had to worry about weight gain, I wanted the hourglass figure. I wanted to be curvy and sexy. I wanted the attention that other girls received. I became obsessed with having long flowing hair, considered breast augmentation and just basically was focused on attaining the ideal acceptable look. The problem with this was that every time I looked in the mirror I was disappointed because what was reflected back was so far from that image. The turning point for me came when my marriage ended and I felt ready for a makeover and (yes, you guessed it!) I cut my own shoulder length hair into a chic short style. The transformation was amazing. I had bought into the idea that long hair is more beautiful and did not realize that for my facial structure short hair suited me better. That led me to examine other ideals that I had bought into. Maybe I didn't need to have large breasts and an hourglass figure to be sexy and feminine. That started my work on accepting and loving my looks and my body. Let me tell you, I spent a lot of time in front of the mirror either fully clothed, partially clothed or in my birthday suit. But instead of noticing all of the things that I didn't like, I took note of what I found attractive. Whenever I got a chance, I took time to admire the way that I looked.

Sometimes just changing what you're thinking about while looking at yourself actually changes the way you look. For example, some mornings when I first look in the mirror I see bags under my eyes and I look tired and worn out. But then I'll catch myself and decide to change my thinking from "Dang girl, you look like the walking dead" to "Hey you sexy Nubian Goddess! I love you and you look marvelous Dahling!" And I swear the bags instantly seem to vanish and my skin looks brighter and well rested. Try it, it really works. I kept up this self-admiration and love and before I knew it I was exuding "so much confidence it's scary" according to a friend.

I love my life now. I have a confidence that I didn't have before. I am much gentler on myself, allowing myself to make mistakes and learn from them instead of beating myself up over them. Going through the terrifying, painful ordeals that I experienced are not something that I would wish on anyone but what I do wish for everyone is the opportunity to apply some of the tools that I've shared in order to fall in love with themselves.

I'm enjoying this leg of the race that I'm running. The baton that I carry is one of self-love and acceptance. Now I'm passing that baton to you. Take it and run with it.

CATHERINE M. WHITE

Catherine is a loving mother, Accountant, and Certified Life Coach. She earned her Accounting degree at Central Washington University and has spent the past several years working in the accounting and financial services arena. She chose to start her practice as a Life Coach because she has always had a talent for bringing out the best in others and has been a source of inspiration and support to those around her. She believes people are like diamonds; some have learned how to let their brilliance shine; others are waiting to be discovered. Catherine has a unique gift for helping people find their beauty and strength within so they can shine like the diamonds they are.

www.survivngthefire.com
catherine@survivingthefire.com

EIGHT

....

FINDING GREATNESS
THROUGH DIFFICULTIES

It was two o'clock in the morning and the night was dark and cool. The narrow dirt path between the house and the outhouse was frightening and seemed endless to me as a young child, but the scariest part about having an outhouse for a bathroom was the fear that I would fall in or that the entire structure would collapse with me inside. This wasn't like a 'Honey Bucket' that you would see at a construction site or at a park packed full of people during the annual 4th of July celebration. This was a hand built – with slapped together boards – box sitting on top of a large deep hole.

My family had very little. Few people knew how I lived as a child because it was not something I would brag about to my friends or classmates. I grew up wearing hand-me-downs and handmade clothing. There were many times we lived without running water or electricity. My parents bought very few groceries from the store; most of our food came from the sweat of our brow because that's all we could afford. I was embarrassed by the way we lived, but most of the time I refused to admit to myself that we were poor. I refused to allow myself to accept that we were so different from everyone else.

I hated my life. I was ashamed of who I was, how I looked, how I felt, and how I lived. I always had friends because I was kind and accepting towards everyone. Yet I was shy, insecure, and unaccepting of myself. I believed I was ugly, despite being told by others that I was a pretty girl. I felt I didn't measure up to my peers and I was afraid to let most people get too close because I didn't want them to know my life.

The Turning Point

My parents separated when I was ten and my mother was pregnant with child number eight. Two years later, my mother made a decision to go back to college and finish her degree which she had started years before and quit once she got married. We moved hours away from the area I had lived in since I was two years old, leaving friends and everything I had grown accustomed to. I entered Junior High that year feeling very lonely. On the first day of school, I made a decision that changed my life.

It was lunch time. I was standing outside near the building watching with envy as the other students ran around laughing and squealing, excited to be with friends they hadn't seen during the summer months. I stood in fear of speaking to anyone. I remember telling myself I could just stand there by myself and continue to be lonely because I didn't know anyone, or I could muster up the courage to go meet someone. After some contemplation, I shrugged my nervousness aside, stepped out of my comfort zone of isolation, walked over to another girl who had been sitting alone, and introduced myself. She invited me to sit next to her and we conversed with each other. The next thing I knew, she was surrounded by several of her friends who quickly became my friends too.

I was not miraculously transformed overnight. However, my decision to break out of my shell of shyness and insecurity boosted my self-esteem and the next few years felt amazing! Although I had my main group of friends who I connected with, I slowly became comfortable associating with nearly everyone in my classes – from the bookworms to the cheerleaders and jocks. The decision I made on that first day of Junior High to break free of my insecurity was life changing as my confidence improved and I began to see myself in a different light. From there on out I continued on a self-confidence building cycle; the better I felt about myself, the more I attracted other people. The more others were drawn to me, the more my confidence grew.

Fast Forward to the Present

I am beautiful! I am confident! I am strong! I love who I Am! I LOVE my life!
I started out like the petals of tiny rose bud, wrapped up in my life of problems, hiding away from the world. When I made a conscious decision to step outside my comfort zone and open myself, I blossomed into a beautiful rose. I see my beauty. I love who I am today and I love the life I graciously live. There are still many struggles I face but I confront them with self-assurance, courage, and faith.

Just as my mother had done, I too am raising my children as a single mom. However, I have been able to provide a life for my children much different then what I had lived as a child. I gave birth to my first two of four children while I was in college. I was taking a full time class load, working part-time, raising two babies, and struggling with my marriage. Though it was extremely difficult to juggle everything emotionally as well as physically, I pushed through my exhaustion and finished with a BA in accounting. Graduation day was remarkable as I felt an incredible sense of relief for completing such an arduous undertaking.

Because of the inner strength I developed through my experiences, I am able to do what I need to in order to ensure my children always have clothing on their backs, food in their bellies and a roof over their heads. We have never had to live without electricity or running water and we have always had a REAL toilet. We may not have everything we want but we have everything we need.

What I Have Learned From My Experiences

The difficulty in my childhood didn't end with poverty and insecurity. There were many other problems my family faced, but I choose not to dwell on them. Rather, I chose to appreciate the hardships I went through because they are part of who I am. I value my past because that is what shaped me into who I have become. My childhood experiences taught me that I had a choice – I could either let my circumstances tear me down or I could use them to mold me and build me into something greater.

I learned that I love to push myself out of my comfort zone and I constantly seek opportunities to do so because I know each time I do, I grow and become stronger. Our comfort zone is our worst enemy because we can be comfortable being miserable. For many people, the idea of change seems far scarier than the misery they currently live in so they stay in the "comfort" of their misery. I choose the path of change daily because I have realized the act of changing is really much easier and the results are far more enjoyable than remaining stagnant where I am.

I learned that if I want something, I have to go for it! I am in charge of my life. I am in charge of my future. It is up to me to create the life I desire – no one is going to do it for me.

I learned good work ethics and how to earn my own money from a young age. I was eager to have money to buy my own things, wear clothing of my own choosing, or go to the movies with friends. Before I was old enough to have a job, I would help my mom do housecleaning for her friends and sometimes they would give me a little money of my own. I quickly understood the power of having my own money and by the time I was twelve I made flyers offering babysitting services and posted them all over my apartment complex. At the age of thirteen, I took on another income source delivering newspapers. I would get up at 4:30 in the morning, seven days a week and walk nearly two hours through rain and snow. When I was old enough to get a "real" job during high school, I did. I used part of my earnings to do things with my siblings – like taking them to the county fair. I enjoyed giving them the opportunity to do things I couldn't do when I was young.

I learned to have love and compassion for others, regardless of their circumstances. Everyone is important and has special gifts or talents. I appreciate the uniqueness that we all have. It is this individuality that makes life interesting.

I learned to love myself and to love my life. The more I loved myself, the more love I could give others. The more love I am able to offer, the better I feel about who I am.

I came to better understand my circumstances, the reasons I have the struggles I do, and have learned to find the blessings in my trials. Earlier this year I was in an automobile accident. Although my injuries were minor, my vehicle was totaled and the insurance settlement was not enough to purchase another vehicle that would properly fit my family. I had plans to buy a house and didn't want to hinder my ability to qualify for a mortgage by taking out an auto loan so I downsized from a minivan to a two door car which had mechanical problems and didn't always run. I grew frustrated with the vehicle and found myself stranded on a couple of occasions. As I wondered if I had made the right decision by purchasing the car I reminded myself that I was making a sacrifice for something better, for my family in the future. I knew I was fortunate to have a vehicle and everything would work out for the best, so I remained steadfast and held to my plan.

Two months later, I lost my home, family pets, and many of my family's belongings in a fire. Many comforts my family had grown to know were suddenly seized from us. We felt robbed of our belongings and were distraught over the many things that were destroyed. The realization that I was so close to losing my children and my own life was horrifying yet I couldn't help but feel immense gratitude for being protected. My family of six (consisting of my four children, a sister, and myself) downsized from a large four bedroom, two bathroom house, to a small two bedroom, one bathroom house with two of us sleeping in the living room. When I received the settlement from my renters insurance, I bought a minivan for my family. It was an incredible feeling to have been able to pay cash for a vehicle and know that I had not risked my opportunity to buy a home. As I drove home in my new van, tears of gratitude poured down my face as the events of the previous months flooded through my mind. The van I bought is newer and has substantially less mileage. It will be much safer and more reliable than the van I had before the accident. It has been six months since the auto accident and four months since the fire. I am now getting ready to close in on my first home purchase.

I learned how to stand strong despite the continual challenges in life that try to knock me down. Through every trial, there is something for me to learn, whether it is faith, patience, tolerance, or love. I have the power to conquer my challenges, and when I do, one or more areas of my life improve.

I have learned to look past the painful thorns of a rose bush and find the beauty of the life that surrounds me.

Find the Roses in Your Life

Just as I have, you too can rise above your circumstances. You WILL be more than you are. Seek opportunities to push yourself out of your comfort zone. Choose good things in life; set your sights high. Establish goals and then work toward achieving those goals. Have love and compassion for others regardless of their differences. Appreciate the challenges in life because greater things are ahead. Stand strong despite your struggles. Use your experiences as the fuel to drive you forward toward something extraordinary.

Love your life no matter what your circumstances are because you are, at this very moment, transforming into someone amazing! Love yourself!

Find the roses in your life. Let your bud blossom and appreciate the roses amongst the thorns.

TIM RAHIJA

Tim is an entrepreneur, business consultant, life coach, and co-author of the International Best Selling book *"Living Without Limitations – 30 Stories to Heal Your World"*. He is the Founder & CEO of Dreamscape Mobile Technology. Tim earned the Medal of Valor in law enforcement in 1990, served in the United States Army among his many accomplishments. He earned a B.A. in Human Resource Management from Mid America Nazarene College in 1989, summa cum laude at DeVry University with B.Sc. in I.T. in 2004. Tim's mission is to reach out, connect with people around the world, uplift, educate, inspire, and transform lives.

21st-century-mobile.com
timothy.rahija@gmail.com

NINE

....

MY JOURNEY OF LOVE FOR SELF

What is love of one's self? To me, this question in the past has created some confusion and misconceptions. One such misconception was confusing love for self as a level of vanity and arrogance, being stuck on one's self and caring only for one's self, not being concerned for the welfare of others. I've come to realize that nothing could be further from the truth. Love for self is not the mindset or act of being focused solely on me.

I have had to pause and consider the love I have for a dear family member, close friend, or other, and ask myself several questions. Do I love that person without judgment or condition? Would I do anything in my power to protect and care for that person? Would I want that person to be in the best possible physical, mental, emotional, and spiritual health? Would I want that person to realize the awesome power and capacity they have inside and reach their full, God given potential and be as successful as possible in each and every endeavor they undertake in life? The obvious answer was a resounding yes. I then had to ask myself "Why would I not also do the same for myself as I would for those I love?"

I came to realize that showing me the same level of love, care, and respect that I give to others is as much about respecting myself in that same manner. Love for self is about developing the mindset, taking specific action, and developing specific habits that help and empower me to be at the top of my game in life, playing life full out as a champion athlete, becoming the ultimate me, which in turn allows me to be all the more effective in my relationships in loving, giving, and caring for others. And, it's also very much about creating and living a life by design versus life by default, where I am the master of my own destiny, setting my own course rather than being governed by the winds and forces of the external world.

Love for self is the embodiment of taking care of me and treating my body, mind, and spirit with the utmost care and respect that they deserve. I have learned to recognize that if I am not at my optimal level of health and performance in all parameters of my life, then my own life suffers as a result and I cannot expect to effectively influence and help others. It is imperative to me that I be the shining example to inspire, motivate, and truly help others. When those around me and across the world are able to see the light of love, joy, happiness, and compassion that shines from within me, I then become that bright beacon of love and hope and a mirror of a higher reality within the universe, and an example of what is possible within the infinite power of the human spirit.

In understanding truly what it means to have love and compassion for myself, I've discovered how important it is to understand the nature of the universe that is us and surrounds us, and the role it plays, as love and compassion are the force and experience that affects all that we do. I've learned that contrary to what we've been taught by modern western science from an early age, you and I are not separate from each other or from the world and everything that surrounds us. Quantum physics has proven the existence of the energy field that is the fabric of the universe and connects everything and everyone. It is the container within which all things exist, the bridge between the creations of our inner and outer worlds, and the mirror for our beliefs that is our reality and shows us what we have created. Our thoughts, feelings, and emotions are scientifically proven, digitally measurable vibratory fields of energy that affect every cell in the body, change the essence of our being, our DNA, which in turn physically affects the "stuff" our world is made of. I can testify to that from my own experience through the power of prayer and absolute belief in helping heal myself following my accident in 2010, which was nothing short of miraculous according to my doctors. That vibratory energy is not limited to the body, but extends for many miles beyond where the heart physically resides and transcends time and space. We communicate with and through this field via the language of emotion.

I chose to introduce you to this as I am very passionate about it, and it is integral to our existence and everyday life and is present in all that we think and feel which in turn affects how we develop the love for self and extend that to our love for others. It is through this field that we connect with and attract those things and people that help empower us and also allow us to place our template of love and compassion into the world and beyond. Think of things in terms of energy and vibration, because all that we see, and all that we are IS energy and vibration. There is no "matter" as such. The emotions of love and compassion have a specific, higher vibrational energy level and are what binds the universe according to ancient philosophy. It is in this context that I want to convey what I have learned in understanding the nature of the universe and vibrational energy and our connection to it as we ourselves are nothing more than energy at the most fundamental level.

Now, having set the stage, I'd like to share with you my own personal experience and insights gained in my life's journey. As I stated in the beginning of this chapter, I believe there is some confusion and misconceptions about what it means to "have love for self." To be honest, it was not until fairly recently, with the help of professional coaching that I undertook in the later part of 2013 and am still involved with as of this writing, that I truly learned what love for one's self really is. All of the misconceptions and beliefs I had were all shattered with the learning and realization of what love for self is, and learning the truth of how really simple it is. I have learned in short order is that there is nothing negative about love for myself. It is the essence and foundation of the universe and is the main reason we are here on this earth; to learn love, and that begins with me and you as individuals.

For many years throughout my life, I had never had an is-sue with self-esteem or confidence, as I have done many things and have had numerous significant achievements, and proved my talents and capabilities time and again. I have had the privilege and honor of earning two college degrees and being an honors graduate on more than one occasion. I have had several careers; having served in law enforcement, served in the US Army, worked in the field of human resources, information technology, aviation and have also been involved in various business ventures and have my own business in mobile technology. I have done many great things, but there were also times that were dark and a bit depressing.

As I said, there was no lack of confidence in skills or abilities, but in looking back I have been able to see where there was ignorance on my part of what love for self was and how and why I did things that did not serve me well. One example was a lot of negative self-talk and beating myself up mentally and emotionally when things did not seem to be going right and blaming myself and putting myself down, not feeling worthy or deserving the good things I saw others enjoying in life. That kind of behavior, in my opinion now, is almost more of a self-loathing than self-love.

And, it wasn't confined to just the mental and emotional aspects of life, but the physical as well. I had smoked for years and even had quit several times, but started up again. I was finally able to quit for good as a result of a near death experience in 2010 that left me hospitalized for about a month and got it out of my system with no urge to start again. There were also times over the years that I drank too much and it negatively affected my health and several relationships. And, not that I really became overweight, but I had not eaten as healthy as I could have either and it seemed like I could never get back to a weight that was more appropriate for me, and again that was more of ignorance of certain facts and a lack of determination and consistency.

Not until recently did it all become so clear between coaching and some simple lifestyle changes I made, and it's made a difference in a few short months. After landing a new job in aviation after nine months of unemployment, I made the decision to get back to a gym and start working out again, which I have done consistently since then and do a lot of walking on the job and in my off time. I added a number of dietary supplements, included protein shakes, more fresh fruits and vegetables, cut back on meat, dairy, simple sugars, drinking the appropriate amount of water for hydration, and other good health habits as a matter of how I live my life now. I've also educated myself more in terms of the systems of the body and how they are impacted by what I do and what I put into my body. I have also discovered many wonderful things in gaining new spiritual enlightenment through reading and meditation that have allowed me to transcend old, unhealthy ways and see the world and universe in a whole new way that is helping me to realize my full potential and purpose in life to help others see and learn what I have, and to reach their own full potential and help raise global consciousness and awareness to a whole new level. The world is thirsty for a new level of spirituality and is what I am helping manifest.

Going back to my near death experience in 2010, I was on my motorcycle one evening when struck by a car and very nearly killed, sustaining numerous severe injuries which required several surgeries, and a painful and sometimes difficult recovery. Waking up in the hospital two days later, not knowing how I even got there was a huge shock, but just knowing that I was still alive spoke volumes to me. That experience told me that I still had a purpose and mission to fulfill in life. It also made me extremely grateful and thankful for having a second chance in life, and caused me to re-examine my life, priorities, perceptions, values and beliefs as to what was truly important, and gave me a new found respect, love, and appreciation for life along with a new way of seeing life and the world.

As I have shown, there is absolutely nothing negative or vane about love for one's self. Transcending to a higher vibrational level has allowed me to achieve a level of mastery of self to better serve others so that we all may share a more peaceful, loving world. It is an amazing journey of discovery. I invite you to come and discover the infinite possibilities with me.

LOVE FOR OTHERS

-

OUR INNER CIRCLE RELATIONSHIPS

ANITA SECHESKY

Anita is a Registered Nurse, Certified Life Coach, International Best Selling Author x 3, Speaker, Trainer, Publisher, NLP and LOA Wealth Practitioner, as well as Big Vision Consultant. She is the CEO and Owner of Anita Sechesky - Living Without Limitations. Anita has assisted many people break through their own limiting beliefs in life and business. She has two International Best Sellers and is launching her first solo book "*Absolutely YOU! –Overcome False Limitations and Reach Your Full Potential*" in November 2014. As a professional compiler and publisher, Anita can help you to put your passion on paper.

www.anitasechesky.com
asechesky@hotmail.ca

TEN

....

LOVE FOR OTHERS

OUR INNER CIRCLE RELATIONSHIPS

When we look into the area of love for others, it's imperative to be fully aware that in order to have a relationship with another human being, one must be willing to open up their heart and allow vulnerability to the emotional connection required which allow others to become an extension of who you truly are. Often we can see people, whether they are relatives, friends, colleagues, or other interest groups, represent an exterior facet of our deepest desire to belong and be connected. Yes, there are times that although we are related to these types of individuals, we aren't truly connected. In fact, we are just playing a role of association as there may be negative emotions from past experiences that affect these relationships from being established on a deeper level.

That being said, when we are aware that we cannot change anyone and we can only change ourselves, our true evolution of awareness and appreciation begins. Suddenly we can see how valuable the connections we do have in life really are. Yes, because we are all on a journey, there may have been times that we did not value our relationships for what they were and how they represented themselves in our lives. You see, personal relationships validate our very being and do not judge or disregard our best interests. They just continually empower and educate us to step into the path of our greatest selves ever.

It's because of these personal connections, we are confident to carry on. They surround us like a cushion of comfort in a world that is harsh and cold. Everyone wants to belong, but what does it take to develop these deep emotional soul ties that will be our strength when we are weak, our compass when we are lost, and our affection when we are rejected in the world? You see, many successful people started somewhere when no one knew who they were. They had their moments of anxiety, stress, or discouragement yet they never gave up because when they were ready to let it all go, someone close to them gave them that pat on the shoulder, made that cup of tea, or gave them that inspirational talk. These are the common roles that parents, siblings, spouses, children, mentors or best friends do best. The world does not know or care about you like these people do. They have already invested their time, lack of sleep, finances, dedication, and energy to pour into your dreams and desires just as you more than likely have done for them. This is the difference of inner circle relationships compared to everyone else. You don't need to beg or pay them for their loyalty and support. They will be your greatest fans and although they may let you down at times, don't take offence. They are only human like you and I, so anyone who can tolerate us in our worst possible state of mind, you can be sure will stick around and help you to get through moments of fear of failure or negativity.

For me personally, my inner circle relationships were pivotal in my self-development process which has always been an ongoing aspect of who I am because of how I choose to show up in the world. You see, whether it was my family, spouse, children, or close friends, I highly regarded their opinions and perspectives even though I may not have always agreed. By allowing myself to not become offended so easily by others, I took time to evaluate and examine the process of any offence by others in my life. Choosing to operate from a mind-set of possibilities and unlimited potential strengthened my inner circle relationships. The value that arose enabled me to greatly appreciate how others, who were close to me, actually cared so deeply for my well-being. You will always be surrounded by people unless you live on an isolated island. Everyone has their own lives and activities to keep them busy and involved. However, the individuals that are close to you will need you just as much as you need them. This kind of validity is what empowers you as you progress and evolve into the characteristics that define you as a person.

When was the last time you stopped and thought back to when you were growing up and how your family interactions brought joy and a sense of belonging? Maybe there was a family joke that kept going that related to past memories or maybe there is a love so deep that it brought you through the worst possible experience that you can imagine. These are the bonds that strengthen and grow deeper as the years go on. Nothing can replace this kind of comfort when no comfort can be given. Because we are spiritual beings, we are connected on such a deep level. This is referred to as unconditional love because there is no definitive explanation of what it may consist of. It just means that the relationship between two people, not necessarily romantic, but on the same plane of existence strengthens and supports one another. You can always depend on these people to come through for you. Just as a parent loves their child, so can a friend love their friend.

I encourage you to seriously examine your relationships with your inner circle. As a Registered Nurse, I have personally observed how traumatic it is when family members lose their loved ones, especially when there are gaps in the communication and physical bond of visiting and being present. Many times, I have seen lives that left this world with broken hearts because of family disputes and disagreements. It is a sad thing to see the look in their eyes, worried if their loved ones would come to see them before their departure. Our lives have no guarantees, but we can make the choices to appreciate and place value where it belongs. Once life is over, there are no second chances as we know of.

Love Without Borders

When was the last time you allowed yourself to just fall in "LOVE?"
Were you thinking very hard, or did it just happen like that?
Did you know before you stepped up to the plate what was next?
What happened inside you? Was the feeling intense? Did you know it had to be real?
What made you stop and take a second look? Why were you so surprised when things just made sense?
Are you feeling Empowered? Enlightened? Encouraged? Elevated?
Does everything just come naturally? Was the connection unbelievable? Are you still in denial? Are you still scared of what's happening deep inside?
Are you trying to reason with yourself? Are you still putting things into place or changing your perspective?

Was it sudden or did it just develop in a way that you had no control? Do you still have butterflies? Will you take it for granted and allow anything to just happen or will you nurture it and let it develop into what it is meant to be?

Do you have the patience to stand close and shower it with the love and attention it deserves? How long are you willing to wait? Do you understand the intensity behind the words and emotions? Are you playing games, or are you mature enough to handle the Explosion of Passion that is building up deep inside?

Love can make you rich, break down barriers, destroy hate, change lives, reroute destinies, rebuild nations, empower the weak, enlighten, restore hope, open deaf ears, conquer fears , give vision, save humanity, control the wicked, ignite passions, stop wars, correct mistakes, heal the broken, save the lost, connect the pieces, and restore the years.

Love can seal two lives for all Eternity!!

Love IS the fountain of Youth!

Are you ready to live a life full of "Love without Borders."

Anita Sechesky

I Love Loving You!

When someone chooses not to return our unbiased and pure love, they are only hurting themselves! Love is a strong force of positive healing energy. We cannot choose who we will fall in love with. We just need to let go of all negativity and fear. Every single life experience we have had up to this point of our existence has happened the way it did because, sorry to say, as a result of our own limited beliefs, negative thinking, and actions. We obviously cannot change the past unless we have a time travel continuum machine! So therefore we need to focus on what and HOW we react to...in the NOW! As we put our clear and peaceful focus and energy on our lives in the PRESENT, we will see that our FUTURE will be better than our past. Negative thoughts will only give power to negative situations and we are enabling them to have a life of their own. BUT...if we consciously choose to be POSITIVE and only look at life this way, we are POWERFULLY making a decision to never be disappointed because LOVE is the universe and it needs LOVE just as we need LOVE to survive. We will always get what we put out in the universe. So what if they don't or won't love you back? At least you are open to LOVE and love will find you! LIKE attracts LIKE. You really need to ask what you are attracting into your life. We can address what needs to be addressed at the moment. But don't dwell on bad things, they will only drag you down and take away from your JOY and positive experiences! All the universe wants to do is bring to you and me that which has always been – all good and for our own happiness. It's all about our choices. Then the universe will not be getting anymore mixed messages, but it WILL all be good.

Anita Sechesky

Hearts in Your Hands

When was the last time you felt special? When was the last time someone made you the center of their universe and trusted only you? When was the last time you felt special?

When was the last time you were kissed in such a way that the whole world faded into space? When was the last time you gave your whole heart, holding nothing back?

Did you try to change the little things that you thought were wrong about you? Did you try to please and please the person you longed to belong to? Did you try to forget about the pain they caused you? How do you trust someone who tells you to open up your heart, only to have them slowly tear it all apart? How do you become brand new when all you see are the wounds that remain?

Do you always forgive when the going gets hard? Do you only forgive because it is the one way to live? Do you change the memories that have left so many awful scars?

I heard so many stories of so many lies. I heard that these lies go on and there is no guilt – there is no remorse.

I heard it is the way of life for so many who are abusers of so many special hearts. I also heard that those who have been hurt will only know hurt and continue the cycle of pain!

Love is not weapon, yet loving someone who doesn't care can sometimes make it feel like a crime.
Love is not a sickness, yet love sometimes makes you want to lose your mind.
Love is not a choice, yet love makes some behave like they have no spoken voice!

How does one go on?
How does one hold on?
How does one forget?

I believe that love is not an oppression. It heals and it reveals. Love is a passion. It's a force that cannot conceal the changes it makes when it is for real.
The tears that have been cried cannot help to dry these special, delicate, and loving eyes.
But God's love is pure and it fills the universe with hope for a love as precious as you are!
Love in the purest form: look at baby creatures big and small. They need love and attention to grow into the creations that they are!
Your life is a gift! Life does go on, and heartaches make us strong. We learn to forgive, let go, look past, and carry on.
I hope that one day, the breakers of these damaged hearts will realize the pain they have caused and learn to never harm any other precious, lovely hearts.

Life has a funny way of showing you how special you are. It may not happen right away, but when it does, you STOP...and realize you have grown and changed!
No more tears; no emotional outbursts.
No more gloomy thoughts of life without "them".
There is something to be said about our precious little hearts. If we let it run its course, even a horrible heartbreak that once crippled you in tears will heal, and you will look back after all the years.
Our hearts are more resilient than we realize because our hearts love us more than we even try.

So give your broken heart a chance to grieve. Let it release all that negativity and soon you will realize you have room enough...to love once more.

Don't become that Heart of Stone. Please don't grow cold! You are only hurting yourself dear one. You are only losing out!

The Heart has a mind of its own. Don't you know we never choose who we love?

We can only follow the beating of our heart! Love will always make this world go around.

A world without love is like a dark, bleak, cold planet without life!

Choose to Love, not hate.
Anita Sechesky

ELIZABETH A. PENNINGTON

Elizabeth is a Certified Life Coach, two time International Best Selling Author, Speaker, Trainer and Mentor. Elizabeth co-authored *"Living Without Limitations – 30 Mentors to Rock Your World"*. She achieved her second Best Selling Author status in Anita Sechesky's second compilation *"Living Without Limitations – 30 Stories to Heal Your World"*. Elizabeth is also a member of the International Coaching Federation. She received her coaching credentials from the School of Coaching Cognition and serves as a coach on Coaching Cognition's platform. Elizabeth offers her clients a safe place to find balance embracing life one step at a time building self-confidence to live life as they desire.

www.theagetolearn.com
eapennington@outlook.com

ELEVEN

....

ENDLESS LOVE

My definition of love is: forgiving. Forgive your enemy regardless of stones thrown into your pathway. Love yourself by first forgiving yourself. Love is taking time to recognize what is in your path of life and embracing it. Love comes with knowing you belong. To belong is to know you are worthy.

I have heard people say keep an open mind. My interpretation of this is: to keep an open mind is to keep an open heart.

Giving love is being there for others. Show kindness or merely say hello with a genuine smile when you meet people throughout your daily routine. This is not to be confused with being polite. Love is powerful and must be exercised.

When you have not stopped to "smell the roses" and refuse to release hurt and pain, you will have placed limits on your heart and mind to receive or give love. When love is not in your heart, happiness becomes limited. Happiness comes from within, from loving our self. Love our self for who we are and for what we stand.

Love is a mystery that gives us the feeling of the highest of highs or brings us to our knees. Love can turn your world into fear or give you security. Love can break your heart or bring laughter. It takes all sort of love to make the world go round. Enjoy the ride.

This chapter is written from not only experience as a life coach but also from personal experience. I have written from the love in my heart, the love of life, and the love for others.

I'm blessed with a special sort of love; one that is there for me when I lose my way and when I'm down in the dumps to pick me up. The gentle love that is there when I believe I have no love left to give and to dance when I do. The love that is there when all else has failed. I dedicate this chapter to the one person who has given me confidence, strength, and encouragement to follow my dreams. I dedicate this chapter to my husband Ronnie.

As a life coach I have had clients who struggled with the meaning of love. Love in a relationship, love in family circumstances, and trying to love oneself when judging themselves as not being worthy.

While struggling with the same love circumstances, I understand how your heart feels torn into many pieces. Sometime the hurt can make you think you cannot go on living. Having wisdom to release the hurtful part of love life dishes out comes from forgiveness, experiencing love which makes your heart overflow with joy and happiness, and keeping an open mind to everything that is possible. For instance, watching a sister return to life from the clutch of death, spared through the power of love.

One client referred to love as a roller coaster with peaks and valleys. I agree love is full of highs and lows! From personal experience, it takes peaks and valleys to teach us appreciation of love. Our lives are full of both cruel and wholesome events. We can become out of balance letting the cruel events override the wholesome events. Choosing to let love into our heart, and forgiving, will help balance life to create happiness.

A personal experience with infertility walked me through a path of the hardest sort of love. While my fiancé and I planned our future I became confused and shocked when my future mother-in-law made a point to tell me I would never be happy married to her son. When I ask why she would say something like that she replied, "He will never be able to give you all you need and you will never have children." I felt so hurt, not for myself but for my fiancé. I loved him so much and could not believe anyone, particularly a mother, would say such a thing. I replied, "You have no clue what I need and we can adopt". She promptly told me she would never accept an adopted child into the family.

My fiancé had been totally honest with me from the start of our relationship. He told me of a disease he had survived but which could possibly cause problems in conceiving. He also explained his mother, due to the illness, decided he would never be capable of having a "normal" life. She would not let him learn to drive nor do other things teenagers do. She never gave him a chance, constantly telling him he would never amount to anything. I had fallen in love with a very different person; an intelligent and loving person. He was a person deserving a chance to be all he could be. I was determined to prove her wrong.

Once married, we decided to wait at least five years before considering children. We worked and lived, enjoying and loving each other for six years. We never gave a thought to the possibility of not having children in our life. Besides, we did not marry just to have children; we married to live our lives together.

After another five years of waiting for nature to take its course, it became obvious we would need to seek professional medical help. For the next three years we tried multiple treatments, but unfortunately none were successful. We talked adoption as an alternative and once again were told an adopted child would not be accepted as a member of their family. We let negative attitudes stop us from adopting and having "our" family.

We accepted the fact we couldn't have children or even adopt a child. We chose instead a life loving each other and have been quite happy with our decision.

Along our pathway of life, we experience feelings of love through joy and hurt. Examples of love from joy may come from the birth of a child, getting our dream job, or finding your true soul mate. A dysfunctional marriage, loss of a loved one through death or separation, or abuses of many kinds are examples of love from hurt. Unfortunately, these kinds of love from hurt may cause us to shut love out.

Depending on the circumstance we could feel shame, rejection, or various other negative feelings. These feeling may cause us to become withdrawn, not letting love in. We have the fear of receiving the same outcome: hurt. Not letting love into our life keeps us from giving love for the same reason. We give love yet receive hurt, so we stop giving and then we start to exist only, not live! We become hardened to the thought of love and life in general.

When we experience love through the joys of life we are on top of the game and the world is in our control. This path must include forgiving those that have wronged us, showing love instead of hate, putting the past to rest, and seeing the true meaning of a happy life.

I've experienced, as most have, loss of siblings, parents, grandparents and friends in death. I've given love and friendship to have none returned. I've been lead to believe I was a friend or was loved only to learn it had been for their convenience.

As a young child, I remember thinking everyone loved everyone else. I did not know hate until my teen years. Then I began to see how people used each other to make gain for themselves at the cost of the other person's feelings. It became clear how a chain reaction to the rest of your life begins.

Having been attracted to and becoming friends with people who seem to always have drama in their lives for attention or those not so popular I received criticism. People told me making friends with their "type" would pull me down and cause me hurt. I suppose I was attracted to them because for many years I hid behind a false face of pretense. It was one of happiness while all the time yearning to have a sense of belonging, the need for security, and the need for understanding. My own feelings and desires gave me the wisdom to understand them rather than to judge them. After years of "fitting" in I realized if my friends were going to walk away because I was acquainted with someone needing friendship and love then maybe it was them who were not friends after all.

Love of life began to change its meaning for me while I was giving my respects at the funeral home. A friend's father had passed away and I was there to support the family during their loss. As I made my way to the chapel, I noticed an open door to a different chapel. At first glance, it looked empty but it wasn't. The deceased was an elderly lady and there were no visitors. I could not get the vision out of my mind or the feeling of loneliness. I return to my friend's chapel, walking to the front and sat down. While sitting there one of the funeral home directors came in and asked if I had known the elderly lady. I replied no. I asked the director why no one was there for her. He replied she had no family left and had no friends. My heart was breaking as I could see myself in her place one day. I was asking myself if there would be anyone there for me. Before the director left the room he said to me, "It is mighty nice of you to be here for this lady when you didn't even know her."

Realizing that night how we all need love in our life, the kind of love that holds kindness, concern, and caring for others instead of hate opened my heart as it did my mind. We need more of the kind of love that can forgive and go on loving even after being hurt. From my own experience you cannot let love in when you cannot give love.

Sometimes you have to possess the strongest sort of love; the love to let go. In this type of circumstance, it is our heart and mind alone that must make the decision as to what is right and wrong. Recently I had to make this choice. Someone very special to me chose a life I no longer could be a part of without causing hurt. They had to make a choice between myself and another person due to jealousy. My love for this person would not let me continue to see and feel the pain the circumstance was causing. It was the hardest decision I have ever made. I walked away but will forever hold love for them in my heart.

The events I have written about involve different kinds of love and have made me what I am today. They have pulled me down, built me up, broke my heart, and made me smile. My many journeys with love have made me a stronger and wiser individual.

Life deals us happiness, sadness, pain, fear, hate, and love. How we handle our life is our choice. If we choose to live in sadness and pain, we become soft. If we choose fear and hate we become hardened to life. If we choose love we change the path of life to happiness. I choose to forgive those that have wronged me. I have chosen love.

If you do not have love in your heart, my wish for you is someday you will find love. Keep both your heart and mind open to the possibilities. Don't close them before taking the chance. Love is a roller coaster and one wonder ride.

Love has no east, west, north, or south. It has no boundaries. When given the chance, love is endless.

HALYNA CHEVPILO

Halyna is a successful entrepreneur, VP of Business Development at Dynamo Entrepreneur, creator of My Academy Of Happiness and holds a BA in Economics. Halyna has overcome many challenges, and obstacles. By believing and staying true to herself, and sticking to her core values of love, happiness, and abundance in life, she has always been able to move forward. Halyna currently lives in Toronto Canada, is a mother of three wonderful children, and the loving wife of an amazing man, the love of her life for the last 23 years. Halyna has a big vision for projects, and ideas to help others to achieve the life they desire. #PeaceAndLove

HalynaChevpilo@gmail.com

TWELVE

....

T H A N K   Y O U   W I T H   L O V E

O nce upon a time in a beautiful city by the lake, there was a little girl sitting on the porch of a house. She was one of those rare souls who was always smiling and happy. She was like a ray of sunshine always brightening up a room whenever she entered. She was always able to see the positive in any situation and this attribute served her well throughout her life, whether it was used when dreaming big or always being able to pick herself up and move on when things looked hopeless.

I feel very fortunate that I was able to reconnect at some point in my life with that little girl and recharge myself again with positive energy, love, and self-healing, understanding my life's purpose and seeing the beauty in each and every single day.

If we take a look at any life story we will see many positive and negative sides. Whether that life story seems more optimistic or pessimistic really depends on how we choose to look at it. Life provided me with a vast variety of experiences to learn and grow from - love, joy, tears, disappointment, happiness, betrayal, new life celebrations, and death of loved ones.

Many times I would go back and relive the past trying to find answers for many questions such as "Was that the life I wanted to live? Did I handle that situation properly or was there a better way? Why did that happen to me?" And I came to realize that it is what it is. I just have to leave it there. Take what I liked and could learn from and move on, living in the present.

I want to share with you my life story from a positive point of view. That's how I see life now. No matter what happened in the past, I treat it as a positive experience and take only good energy to my present and future. That's how I practice living happily and in abundance every day. I find small things to energize my day – kissing my kids in the morning, enjoying a good chat with my husband, saying hello to my social media friends, or even smiling to people on the street.

My life story is centered around special relationships with loved ones and the many experiences, both negative and positive, that we experienced together. Having someone to share good and bad times with makes life experiences either more bearable or more enjoyable. I'd like to share some of these stories with you and the special place that my loved ones hold in my heart in the form of letters which I wrote a few years ago.

Letter to my dear husband:

We have been on our life journey together for over twenty years and I want to say that you are not only an amazing man but also an amazing human being. I've loved you from the first moment that I saw you. I know that it sounds strange how we just got married after knowing each other less than three months. But I strongly believe that if it is meant to be you will feel it...time is not a sign but emotions are.

I remember the joy and overwhelming happiness we felt when we found out that we were expecting our first baby! It was wonderful and surreal to feel and experience the beginning of a new life!

Do you remember the first week we brought our precious son home? That was a totally new experience for both of us! You were always there by my side, helpful and loving!

I cannot forget the warmth of your hands holding my hand after the surgery when we lost our second unborn baby. I was also thirty minutes away from losing my life. That was the most heart-wrenching period in my life. I felt that I lost a part of me and I would never be the same. Even now, writing this letter, the tears are running. That pain would never have subsided without you being on my side. You are my rock.

A few years later life presented us with another challenge and bump to overcome. I had to leave you and our son and go to another country. Ever since I was a little girl I wanted to move to Canada and I remember deciding with my cousin that one day we would live there. Law of Attraction was at work and here I was getting my wish. However I had to leave my two loves and it felt like the longest six months of my life having to wait for you to join me.

Six months was nothing however compared to the five years that we had to wait to bring our son over to our new country and home. It was a heart crushing experience with 1825 days of crying. Thank you my love for staying strong, keeping my faith up for a positive ending, having a clear vision and manifesting the results we needed.

The joy of finally having our family together and a new home was fantastic!
I am very proud of our son, who was dedicated to school and sports, and looking at him today we both have hearts filled with joy and gratitude. I am blessed to be a mom and your wife. Love you my love.

My favorite quote – *"I am realistic and I am expecting miracles."*

Our first miracle came almost seventeen years later when, against medical odds of getting pregnant because of the past surgery, we gave a birth to beautiful baby boy! Wow!!! Life was beautiful every day!!! I would never have expected twenty years ago that, being over the age of thirty-five, I could have a child. But that was not all. Within a year and a half we were blessed with a baby girl! That's what I called a double miracle!!! When you are in love all is possible. Love you.

Having two young children at this stage of my life was a welcome life experience. I viewed the sleepless nights and crying babies as signs of joy and happiness. Honestly darling, keeping up with kids all day with their bursts of energy and desire of adventure makes me feel fifteen years younger.

With your help I've learned to enjoy what we have been given by life, good luck, and miracles. The Rule of Universe is to enjoy and appreciated what you have and you'll get more. Give without asking for anything in return.

I love you...I know and feel that you love me ten times more.

Letter to my parents:

I am very happy that at this point in my life I have stopped playing the blame game and I am thankful to have you as my parents. I'm also grateful for what you've done to help me be who I am. Thank you for stepping in and helping to raise our son when we couldn't be there and also for helping us when we lost everything and had to start over.

I know that neither one of us are perfect and at the end life is not about perfection – it's about accepting who we are without pretending and it's never too late or too early to learn to be a better person.

Love you Mom and Dad!

Letter to my beautiful children:

I've loved you from the moment that I became aware of your existence and couldn't wait for you to arrive. As you grew, we watched in awe and delight as you took your first steps and said your first words. Nothing could have prepared us for the amazement as we noticed the resemblance between you and either myself or your father when we were your ages. It's so simple yet powerful how nature and love creates human beings.

Quite often I've looked back in the past and wondered if I could have done more for you or done things differently, reacted calmer, or gave you better advice. But on the other hand, at the time I felt that I was doing the best that I could. It was always my intention to be the best mother to you. We grew and learned together each day and unfortunately there was no manual to use or instructions to follow. The main thing is the love. Love was always at the forefront, even if it wasn't said out loud. I love you with all my heart and always will.

I tried to raise you kids with the right to have certain freedoms and yet still be disciplined. I tried to respect your opinions and tastes and to always be ready to give advice and show support when needed. I always wanted to value you as important people in my life.

I always respect your reason for tears and will try not to provoke them. When you have tears, my heart wants to bleed.

A mother's life and mind revolves around her children and no matter what I do in life, I have you in mind. You are the center of my Universe and my reason to live a good life and move forward. I know that it might sound strange to you, but you will understand that one day.
Love you now and always, Mom

Letter to my sister:

I have been told many times that I am blessed to have my sister here in Canada, and I truly am!

I am grateful to have you in my life. I remember my relatives asking me when I was seven years old whether I wanted to have a brother or sister. I said, "Hmmm, I am ok by myself". A few months later I got you, my little baby sister!

I always remember when mom asked me to take you outside to play. I was wondering when you were going to grow up. Time passed quickly and you grew up into the best sister anyone could ask for. You've always been there for me filling my life with light and happiness.
Love you my sis!

Letter to my friends and all the people in my life:

Love you all!
I'm so happy to have you in my life and to learn from you. I'm happy to help you whenever and however I can. We all here for reason and my reason is to share with you love, happiness, and joy!
#PeaceAndLove
Yours, Halyna

I now live in a state of happiness and in the faith that tomorrow will be a new magical day. I strongly believe that we are creators and magnets for good things to come into our lives. We are very unique and special guests in this universe so we have to be treated well! We are powerful and in control of what we want to have and achieve, and by believing and taking action and being guided by our hearts, we can create our desired results. My life is fantastic and I want to keep it fantastic – that's my goal! I am the messenger and my message and mission is to tell you that you are beautiful and never alone in this world. In those times when you feel alone and it seems as if no one cares, send love to the universe and ask for help and advice. Just ask. The answer will come in some form or sign.

We have to use more positive words and take more action towards our well-being. The power is in us. Don't wait for some big snowball of happiness to show up in your life one day so you will live happily ever after. Happiness is built every day from within, from your heart, soul, and your beautiful mind. Open your eyes and see the world with love and passion. Practice good thoughts each day. It will become your daily habit and you will love yourself and world around you.

BARBARA JASPER

As a Mompreneur, Barbara has 23 years of corporate, entre-preneurial and entertainment experience working with brands like Time Warner Cable, Chapters/Indigo, Girl Guides of Canada, and MuchMusic to name a few. She's used her years of relationship marketing knowledge to create successful new ventures breaking through start-up barriers fast and with style. She's a social media maven and most notably co-founded and launched a National Girls Empowerment Magazine in three months and co-founded and launched a Global Women's Empowerment community and successful online/YouTube show in two. Barbara and her husband, Lee, have three children, Christopher, Jessica, and Natalie, and have been happily married for 27 years.

barb.jasper@rogers.com

THIRTEEN

....

A REAL LOVE STORY

February 14th, 1986. Valentine's Day.
I was on a lunch break from the new temporary job I would be working at for the next two weeks when flowers arrived. They came addressed to "Barbara" with a blank note card. What happened next changed my life. The card was removed and the blank space was filled with, "*Welcome to the company*" along with three names signed. How nice! These guys were welcoming me? Ha! Can you spell g-u-l-l-i-b-l-e? I thought I was receiving a random act of kindness but I was just the target of a prank. Funny guys...real funny. It would be months before I found out this was part of a plan to win my affection.

Two months later I was on the best first date, ever. One of the pranksters and I went to dinner and a club. When there was nowhere else to go that was open after hours, we sat in the car listening to music until the sun came up. Oh, what a night! We repeated that every night after for a week. We had a whirlwind romance of wining, dining, dates, and parties. Promises were made to be together, forever in love. We would spend hours talking and we couldn't get enough of each other. We often spoke of a future together, and on Christmas morning, only 8 months later, he proposed marriage and I said, "YES!" On September 26th, 1987, a year and a half after we met, we were married.

The first two years were spent traveling the world. We experienced Hong Kong and China, we skied the best resorts in Canada, and we wined and dined at the bullfights in Spain. We soaked up the sun and enjoyed fancy drinks on some of the nicest beaches in the world. We were in love and life was good. No...scratch that; life was GREAT!

For a few years after that, our life was amazing. We had a beautiful home filled with kids, teddy bears, and toys but all the while I was having serious health issues.

It's at this point that I'm going to make a leap...forward in time through all the pain, the fighting, misinformation, and diagnosis...to the point in the story where trying a last-resort effort in the form of a chemically-induced pseudo menopause left me chemically depressed for years. I was alone and hurting. Thoughts of apathy and suicide filled my days and I often cried myself to sleep when no one was looking. "What's wrong with me?!" I was full of anger and rage, I didn't know why, and I couldn't control it. My husband loved me but he didn't understand. And neither did I. He couldn't fix it and so he was mad - at me or because of me. I didn't know. It didn't matter. We fought, a lot. All we could do to end the horrible days was kiss good-night and say, "Tomorrow's a new day." "Good-night beautiful," he said. Always. I could look awful with a messy head, a runny red nose, and be in the same pajamas for days and he'd still call me "beautiful". After six weeks of pneumonia I can tell you, I didn't feel beautiful. Pneumonia was the respiratory condition I got two, three, and even six times a year. It started with me in my 20's and was in 2001 that it stopped and never had ailment since then.

"Good news – you'll never have pneumonia again. Bad news – you have cancer; lung cancer. Let's do the surgery in 3 weeks." Sucker punch to the gut. "What did you just say?!"

My kids were playing in the corner with their toys, oblivious to what just happened. They were six, nine, and ten years old, and they were happy. They had no idea their lives just changed forever. I asked the most important question, "Am I going to die?" People don't survive lung cancer. The doctor scheduled my surgery for two months down the road and then sent me home – dismissed as if I was told about the results of a strep throat test. Really?

Home. Everyone was mad. Mad at what was happening, at each other; fighting. I was fighting to be heard, for understanding, for my life. Fighting my husband to make him understand I didn't hear things wrong. I was fighting to hold back tears. "I'm going to die". Fighting. The whole night fighting. We got through the night and made it to bed, mad, sad, scared and angry. I got my usual kiss. "Good-night beautiful." This time though he added, "Don't worry, we'll get through this. Everything will be fine." Yeah, right.

On May 23rd, 2001 I went into the hospital, but not before I wrote my family their good-bye letters. I put them in the filing cabinet with all the bills so when my husband had to finalize my things, he'd find them and they would know how much I loved them. The house was clean so he didn't need to do that before my funeral. Did he know I liked flowers, that my day should be filled with them, and that they should all get buried with me? I forgot to tell him that. I wonder if he knew that I wasn't coming home. He stayed right by my side until I fell asleep, drugged by anti-anxiety medication. I didn't want to die. I said "Good-bye" as they wheeled me away.

I woke up and saw him crying. "You're awake". I was in the I.C.U. I was on morphine for pain. There was a nine-inch scar on my back and I had eighty staples holding me together, literally. I had no idea that day was the easy part.

Home again. What just happened? Nothing about my life made sense. The only thing I knew was that I couldn't lean on my husband. I was alone again. He was now the mother, father, chef, bread-winner, referee, and everything in between. He had enough to deal with; he had his own fight. He shouldn't have to take on any more, you know? He tackled his relegated roles with zest and humor, and while I resented his approach, it would prove to be the ONLY thing that got us through the next few years. Love and humor. Who knew *that* would be our salvation? "Good-night beautiful."

For months and years, while I was physically healing, I was mentally falling apart. By now I had pushed away most of my friends and no one understood. How could they? I didn't. I shouldn't be here. Finding my cancer was an accident. I would have died. I shouldn't be here! What happened to my life?

I saw Psychotherapists, Psychiatrists, and went to support groups to find healing. I'm not sure I ever did. I wasn't a typical cancer patient and so empathy and sympathy were hard to find. I didn't look sick, so people thought I shouldn't act sick and questioned if I really was. "Who has cancer and no chemo or radiation?" were questions I got asked. No one, other than my husband knew my real pain and struggle. And some days I hid it from him because it was easier to have him mad at me for having another bad day than to explain how I was really feeling. I was ridiculed and belittled, and hurt. Eventually, personal therapy sessions led to opening up wounds from years gone by that I thought I dealt with and so healing from cancer opened other wounds that would take more than 12 years to heal. I wandered through my life working, volunteering, serving, and helping others (and doing a fine job of it, by the way) all while trying to figure out how to survive. If I couldn't help myself, then at least I could love someone else and make their day better. Yup, that's what I'll do.

I would have major successes and even win awards for my efforts. There was no pattern to when the bad days came and every time it happened, it hit me hard. But always by my side was my husband; my silly, goofy, irritatingly funny husband. "Good-night, beautiful".

Now don't get me wrong, this is *not* a fairytale. Our marriage was tested, but that's not my point; *Love* is. It does conquer all. We're living proof of that. Cancer was the single most tragic thing to ever happen to our family and love saved us.

You don't know how strong you are until that's your only option. Some days I fought valiantly with dignity and grace, and others I crumbled under pressure. One New Year's Day I remember I was paralyzed, crying and feeling sorry for myself. Nothing changed with the ringing in of a new year. His reaction (as mad as I was to hear it at the time was exactly what I needed), "You're either living or you're dying. Pick one!" That day I picked myself up off the couch, wiped my tears and chose living. It's not always pretty, but I'm doing it.

Even though I woke up on May 23rd, 2001, I died. The Barbara pre-surgery is gone, but my husband's love and commitment to our family's recovery has allowed me to heal while being a full-time mom, volunteer, and entrepreneur. We've sacrificed things for experiences, and we're okay with that. Our day always ends with, "Good-night, beautiful" and we *always* hug and kiss our kids good-night.

Fast forward again. It's now July 2013 and I'm getting ready for the day. I decided just that morning I would finally tell my story. To that day I hadn't said a word out loud. I've been asked many times why haven't I written a book to tell the story people thought they knew (would you believe there's more?). I packed up my stuff, my courage, and a boxed lunch and left to pick up some gal pals. Off we went to learn and be empowered. All for one and one for all. My husband wished me good luck. "Bye, beautiful. Have a nice day."

Something happened; I found my voice. I learned that day that I am strong; a fighter. Why hadn't I seen before what others had seen in me for years? Doesn't matter. Better late than never, right? I told my story (parts of it, anyways), and there were tears, laughs, hugs and high-fives. The final exercise that day was to cross a line drawn in the sand that represented the old you on one side and the new on the other. I said to myself as I crossed it, "I will NEVER be held back by my story again. I'm changing my life, starting now."

And I have. Through the unconditional love from my husband and kids, my education, and personal growth over the last 13 years, I have reinvented *Barbara*. I am a strong woman who owns her scars and her story. I am not ashamed to say I'm not perfect because it's true. My life has been hard...is hard, just like yours, but it's a real life filled with love.

Being *real* is what it's all about.

To my husband:

You have been the only person in my life who has loved me unconditionally. Neither of us is perfect and when life threw us a curveball (and there have been many), we stuck together, fought, and won. When life got really rough and we fought each other, we always found our way back, and I love you for that; for never giving up on us. I love you not for what you've given me, but for what you've shown me; that love is sharing the good and the bad - together - no matter what.

Thank you for stealing my flowers the very first day we met.

I love you.

COURTNEY WALTERS

Courtney is an aspiring writer who, in addition to being a co-author in *#LOVE – A New Generation of Hope*, is also working on her first non-fiction novel. Courtney completed the Dental Assistant program at Everest College. In her spare time she enjoys mentoring, tutoring adult learners, and is an active volunteer at various food banks in her hometown. Courtney lives in Mississauga, Ontario, Canada with her son.

walters_courtney@hotmail.com
facebook.com/courtney.walters

FOURTEEN

....

MOTHERHOOD CHANGED MY LIFE

Patiently I waited for the results of the home pregnancy test. I sat with the phone to my ear with who could be the father of my child on the other end. Hearing his voice in the distance, I could not focus on what was being said. Staring past the test, my mind was racing..."Am I ready for this? I know nothing about raising a child. Am I really ready to have a dependent?" Hearing my name being called for the fifth time, I finally snapped out of my daze. Preparing myself, I looked down at this stick that now holds my fate. POSITIVE! Oh man...really?! To say I had mixed emotions is an understatement. Happy, scared, and overwhelmed were just a few. All I could think of was how different life as I knew it was about to change.

The next few months were a breeze. My pregnancy was nothing like I expected – no sickness, no pain, and no nothing. Just a lot of attention! All of a sudden everyone wanted to do everything for me. But at the same time this baby had changed me and matured me. I was starting to see life...the real meaning of life, and felt my partner didn't have the same "new life glasses" I had on.

Floating through the pregnancy without a hitch physically was one thing, but emotionally I was trying hard not to let my new found feelings towards my child's father effect my baby or my own bliss. One morning I got the call that shook me to my core. My son's father had been arrested! You're kidding me! This couldn't be happening. I just remember crying. I never thought I'd have to take this journey on my own. Call it wishful thinking or being naive, but not once had it crossed my mind. Now there I was five months pregnant, nineteen years old, still living at home, about to start this life long journey alone!! This situation hit me like a ton of bricks.

The rest of the pregnancy was spent under a mask. I felt that I couldn't completely express my emotions since everyone told me my baby could sense everything I was experiencing. So I locked those feelings away and carried on with a smile. Month by month, seeing less and less of my feet by the week I was anticipating the arrival of my prince. I celebrated my baby shower without my son's father. I concentrated on only portraying my strength and excitement, while hiding from my family members my shame of already being a single parent.

A few weeks before I was due, my son's father had made his return to the free world. Although I was beyond pissed, I was more relieved to not have to go through this alone. We put on this front as if everything was fine and nothing had changed.

My son was born December 8th, 2009. This was the first day of my new life – my new life as a mother. I can't say it was hard. I was one of the fortunate ones who had a lot of help.

I just got to enjoy being a mother watching my son grow. He would look at me with such love in his eyes like he always knew who I was. Here I was floating in never-never land and BAM! Hit with a ton of bricks again!

Once again my son's father was back in prison. This time I fell apart. I had to...I was running out of room to hide all my true feelings. But still I thought it was crucial to make sure my son had a relationship with his father. I did the whole nine yards – the visits behind the glass, the social calls which lasted all day and the trailer visits. To say the least, living like this started to take its toll on me. In the midst of everything I was dealing with in my own family, my mother was selling the house which meant it was time to move out and stand on my own two feet.

There I was. Twenty-one and never had to really pay a bill my entire life up to this point. So I finally put on my big girl pants and moved out. There were times when I would just break down and feel like a failure. I can honestly say the way my son would look at me is what kept me sane. His eyes kept telling me I was his everything and that he loved me no matter what. It's was our way of communicating.

For the next year or so nothing had really changed, for the better or the worst. I constantly found myself battling with the decision to push my feelings aside. After all, this is what everyone is striving for...isn't it? To raise their child in a two- parent household? I had already messed up having a baby out of wedlock. Although it was never that big of a thing in my family, I still hated being a statistic. For some reason I felt staying and trying to make it work and eventually getting married would somehow make people forget I did things a little backwards.

So I continued the cycle of playing house, being there for him while he was incarcerated, and telling my son his father lived in a castle and would one day return to us. It worked for a little while. I'd always joke to myself and say I deserved an Oscar. But as the months went by, this temporary fix wasn't holding up. It was almost like the equivalent to fixing a leak with masking tape! I could almost feel my sanity slipping away from me. Putting everyone else's happiness before my own for this so called greater good was driving me to a place I didn't like. All this for my son...or so I thought that was what I was doing it for.

I finally told myself enough was enough. Watching my son starting to get older and wiser was the push I needed to get my head where it had to be. I set my fears aside and decided to get my life on the track I've always wanted, or at least point myself in the right direction. I wasn't going to sit there and paint a picture as if one day I woke up, got my ducks in a line, and got accepted into college. This is something I'm still working at, long and steady.

It took becoming a mother to start figuring out who I am. And as I said earlier, I don't have everything together, but I'm happier. At times you lose sight of what you want in life. You get into relationships and situations, and there might be some aspects of it that you like. But along good, we tend to accept and down play the bad. It took me four years to realize that it doesn't have to be that way. My son taught me that to be a great mother; I have to be happy with my life. I have to be content with my decisions. The more that I began to think this way the more changes I started making in my life. I started working out and eating better. I had to really take a step back and look at what I was putting into my body and how I was taking care of myself, or should I say not taking care of myself. I remembered back in high school when I was one of the top athletes, what kind of shape my body was in. I had so much energy and felt very strong. But it wasn't that way any longer and that wasn't cutting it. A change was needed. The obvious benefit that others would notice would be a fitter looking me. The other reason was so that I could keep up with my rambunctious active son and instill in him the importance of taking care of oneself. Changing the way that I ate was a bit more challenging. Giving up fast food and soft drinks made a huge difference quickly. But I must be honest, it's not that easy.

Instilling in my son values and beliefs about himself that will help to shape his character and self-image is something that I am passionate about. My mother was a huge proponent of that. She was always telling my brother and I that we can do anything we set our minds to. I remembered when I said that I wanted to be a hair dresser, she immediately commented that I could own the salon, not just work there. I understand what she was doing but honestly back then, it just seemed that everything I wanted to do wasn't good enough. I now know that she just saw unlimited potential in me, and that is exactly what I see in my son. It is an amazing feeling of responsibility when I think of the privilege I have in shaping this little man. I take that very seriously and do my best to make him feel good about himself, and the world. One of the ways I inspire self confidence in him is with a game that we play each day. It is called the "I AM" game. It's a simple game where we take turns making declarations and affirmations such as "I am Smart", "I am important", "I am brave", etc. He has no problems coming up with positive adjectives to describe himself. That is huge and I don't want him to ever lose that confidence.

My son has given me the confidence and reason to go back to school, to hold my head high, and not be ashamed of my past decisions. He gave me the strength and determination to take six different buses to school every morning while I was taking my dental assistant course in college. It forced me to show myself what I could be capable of – if I just believe in myself.

You know, when you have someone who sees you as a heroine, you can't help but feel more powerful and confident. Writing this chapter has caused me to step out of my comfort zone and do something that people around me have been saying that I should've done for years. I've thought of writing non-fiction, and I will write that book one day. But co-authoring in this book is one of the most emotionally draining things that I have done in a long time. Anyone who knows me knows that I'm tough; I don't show a lot of emotions. I'm very good at masking them as I've mentioned before. But writing this has made me dig deep...deep down into the places that I really didn't want to revisit. It has been a battle just getting the words out. I've thought of quitting multiple times but I haven't because I see this as something that I have to conquer. This will be another notch in my belt of things that I've been able to accomplish because I am his hero. Being his mom has given me the combination to unlock hidden strengths that I didn't even know I had.

Making the decision to become a mother was the best thing I've ever done. Learning how to be a great mother is my proudest accomplishment thus far. Because of my son I am who I am today. I might not be where I want to be in certain areas in my life, but being his mother gives me inner joy and peace. Taking this journey, throughout the ups and downs, thinking I wasn't doing a good enough job, wasn't in vain. He's given me a story! A purpose! He's giving me the opportunity to tell my story and hopefully show other young single mothers that it isn't always easy, but it's worth it. I'm by no means a superwoman, but that'll never be something my son would believe. That's what keeps me going.

CHERYL GINNINGS

Cheryl encourages people to "reach for the stars." She graduated Sam Houston Magna Cum Laude with honors degree focusing on how communication breaks down in families with special needs children. While at SHSU, she won many awards for speaking and has published articles and produced a video. Cheryl realized first-hand that we should choose to be better, not bitter, because of troubles. Her special needs son caused her to speak up to open doors for others and not accept failure. As a speaker, minister's wife, and mom, Cheryl has spoken for more than 40 years in many states, Universities, retreats and Bible classes.

cherylginnings@gmail.com
facebook.com/cheryl.ginnings

FIFTEEN

....

A JOURNEY OF A LIFETIME

One important journey in my lifetime began in 1970 with my first pregnancy. I was so excited and expected a healthy baby! But my life took a different direction because my son had health issues. Nurses gave me ether to keep me from delivering my son before the doctor arrived. When he was born I soon realized that the medical staff believed something was wrong with my baby. No one told us he did not breathe right at birth! After hearing other babies being rolled down the hallway to their mothers, the doctor finally told us that our son had turned blue several hours after birth.

What did they think was wrong with my baby? Why wouldn't anyone tell us anything?

After spending seven days in the hospital, I was discharged, not receiving any explanation about my son's health issues. Although he had to stay in the hospital, I was beginning a difficult part of my journey: frustrations, anxieties, unanswered questions, and despondency.

When my son came home, he cried all day and most of the night. He had a peculiar look in his eyes at times; it was hard to describe. He did not nap in the day like most infants and could not keep much of his food down. Weekly we consulted medical doctors because we knew something was definitely wrong with our son. Each doctor kept assuring us that he was healthy and that we did not understand new babies. It was frightening to know in our hearts that he was not "normal", yet no help was available. Our friends and family realized something was wrong before we did. When we told the doctors that he cried all the time, we were advised if we laid him in the bed, he would quit crying within thirty minutes. But he did NOT stop.

After five months of lack of sleep, my health took a dive. While out of town, I became very ill and was taken to my mom's doctor who knew right away that I had kidney stones. I was admitted to the hospital with a 106-degree fever, pneumonia, and septicemia. I became gravely ill and had two surgeries during the following twelve days. While I was in the hospital, my mom took our baby to her doctor. He agreed with her that something was very wrong and sent her to the best neurologist in Nashville. However, this "so-called" specialist told her she was over reacting and she was a smothering grandmother! During the following six weeks of my recovery, I stayed with my parents. When I found out the neurologist wanted to see me, I was upset that my parents had taken our son to the doctor. However, I became more upset when this "specialist" said nothing was wrong, BUT if there was, nothing could be done until he reached school age. Having taught baby classes for years at church, I suffered watching other babies do things ours could not. I knew the doctor was not right!

When I was able to return home, we told our own pediatrician about the neurologist's assessment. Our pediatrician kept an eye on our son and at eight months old, he sent him to Vanderbilt hospital for evaluation. After waiting for six long weeks, we got a letter stating "Idiopathic retardation!" (Translation: we don't know what is wrong or what to do with the baby!)

The first fourteen months were demanding! He "spit up" on me all the time, as the doctor described it, but it was projectile vomiting! He continued crying all night. No matter what we described to the doctor, he reassured us our baby was fine! BUT he WASN'T!

My husband saw I was about to collapse from exhaustion, so he went to our doctor and said, "Either put our son in the hospital, or put my wife in the hospital!" So we returned to Vanderbilt for more tests. This time we got the diagnosis of cerebral palsy and seizures, but no explanation. With medication for seizures, our baby settled down and did not cry. However, I would sleepwalk to the crib, exhausted and dreaming he was crying!

During this time my parents helped us put a perspective on our situation. As they prayed with us at the hospital, they explained that no matter how hard this was to face, physical problems were not as hard to bear as seeing your children have spiritual problems. That has really been true.

I researched to understand what the diagnosis of cerebral palsy meant. The only book I found was written twenty years earlier describing a school in Kansas. We went to visit it. It was like a note from heaven to find a school, a job, and the money for the care all in one day. So, we moved to Kansas willing to do whatever was needed to help him.

After the admitting doctor in Wichita, Kansas, looked in our son's eyes a few minutes, he said, "There is no hope for him. I will suggest the school not take him." How could he say that? We had just moved from Tennessee to Kansas for help. This doctor saw no hope and told us to put him away; forget him and have another baby as soon as possible!! Are babies disposable? Forget one and have another! How cruel! Babies are human beings who deserve better. Special children are people too. My anger subsided and my determination rose as the school accepted him three days a week.

After nine months, my husband got a better job so we moved about ninety miles away. We then drove three days a week for our son to have help. After twenty-two months of commuting, the school told us to either let him live in the school or take him out. What a choice! Although our family was wearing out with the drive, it was a hard choice to make. Our love for our son was so great that we made the decision to keep him home with us. The idea of leaving him there was too hard to do.

Again, God answered our prayers. There was a little school with two teachers who came to our house and explained they did not have all the credentials of the institute we came from but would do their best. And it was great!

After another year passed and our first sweet baby girl blessed our lives. As she grew, she loved her brother. When she was about two, on one of the visits to our home, the two teachers told our little girl that she was our son's best teacher. Although she was four years younger than him, she was demonstrating the movements, language, and curiosity our son needed to see!

When he was about seven years old, I fell off a ladder and severed my heel bone. While I recovered with a huge cast and crutches, our little girl watched our son and helped him get to a sitting position with his legs in the shape of a "W". She encouraged him to follow her. And he did!!! As he worked his way into a sitting position, he would hop with hands in front. She would say, "Come on, Frog!" He would giggle and go faster to keep up with her. Seeing him gain some independence, we laughed as he hopped and followed her up two steps and down the hall.

Our family grew with another baby a few years later. The three would have tea parties with cardboard boxes for a table. Our precious little girls would make up things just his height and they would pretend for hours to cook "chocolate pies" like one grandmother and drink "coffee" like the other grandmother.

There are so many joyful memories of having the children at home. I cherish the fun of trying to learn how to teach our son. I even taught the kids the books of the Bible. If I thought of some crazy way to teach him things, we would actually invent our own special equipment. It didn't always work, but we tried.

Many people are afraid of persons with special needs. I learned so much from having such a special son. I saw him love unconditionally, and we rejoiced over every tiny improvement. When he finally could raise a hand to knock a wooden ring down a rod, we clapped as if he had finished a marathon! Everything he learned was difficult. Therapists worked with him three years to drink from a straw. Our son was eleven when he was finally potty trained. Every step took time, patience, and repetition. We had tutors, occupational, speech, and physical therapy, and homework from all of them. When he was eleven, my health broke down and I had to be cared for. Since he was total care, we realized we could no longer care for our son at home. But I can tell you that there is no bond stronger than a mother's love for her own child. I have been able to see that our son has so much love and charm.

Our family moved a couple of times and each time we had to find help. At one residential facility, a therapist helped him learn to paint and his art hangs in many places from Texas to Washington. He can't handle money, but he handles a paintbrush that pleases many who own his art. On the other hand, we had to deal with horrible situations, including abuse or helpers stealing from him. At one group home, I was so angry when someone assaulted him. I could not allow this horrible situation to continue for our son who could not tell us what happened. Although agencies investigated, I was determined to find another place for him.

In search of a better place for him, I interviewed fourteen facilities in less than a week. It was through this darkness that God opened the door for a sweet young couple to take him into their home with their children and love him. They have the best attitudes with supporting family and friends I have ever seen. This is the first time in my life I could say,

"If anything happens to me, they would take care of him the rest of his life."

Our son loves to Skype, travel to Texas Ranger games, and to see us at home. He loves his family and his family is supportive of him. He surprises us knowing more than we ever thought possible. He charms those who care for him. He loves God like few can.

Even though he is now 44, it is still taxing to get the needed services he requires and deserves. When trying to get the wheelchair he needed, we worked for over four years calling, writing, and returning to the agency with documentation they had misplaced, lost, or discarded. Finally, we received what our son needed for that one item.

Through the many difficult situations our family has faced, our dependence on God and gratitude for answered prayers is stronger than ever. When we faced the most difficult challenges, God provided answers better than we could imagine. It grieves me to hear people blame God, or ask where God was when bad things happened to them. They forget He sent his only beloved Son to earth to die for us. God did not promise our lives would be easy. He promised that He would be with us – no matter what! What more could we ask for in this life?

Without our amazing daughters and our very special son, my life would not be complete! I share my story because there are others who have gone through even more difficult situations than I have and are joyful. God's grace is sufficient to encourage me to never give up. I choose happiness and joy.

LAUREN MILLMAN

Lauren, B.A. Psych, CCF, CCP, ACC, AIC, is Toronto, Canada's highly sought after Certified Coach Practitioner specializing in Relationships and Effective Communication for Women Executives and Entrepreneurs. Since 2004, Lauren has helped thousands of women have more connected and fulfilling relationships, empowered conversations, enriched and meaningful lives. Lauren's approach to Coaching is unique. She has had many of the same issues her clients have, giving her the experience and expertise needed to help through difficult situations, find solutions, and live with peace and happiness. Lauren is a published Author, Speaker, and Asperger's Expert, and the Recipient of the Women in Leadership in Canada Award, 2014.

lauren@laurenmillman.com
facebook.com/LaurenGMillman

SIXTEEN

....

SPRINKLES AND WHIP, PLEASE!

Sometimes, we get to choose. We find ourselves in front of the menu board. We get to choose our exact desires, and we allow ourselves the luxury of contemplating our order. What will make me happy? What will make me feel good? And so, we order, and get exactly what we want. How lucky are we! I like to order whipped cream with sprinkles. That makes me happy. I can live with that.

As parents, or parents-to-be, we don't get to "order off the menu", and we can't pick and choose. We get what we get and we don't get upset. I have three beautiful children, all gifted, and with some unexpected challenges sprinkled on top, just for good measure. I didn't get to choose...and what I got weren't the easiest kids in the world, but they were beautiful. Thank goodness! With my first, he didn't want to eat what we ate. He had a repertoire of five foods; bread, cream cheese, cheese sticks, apple sauce, and one other soft-food item I can't recall. Sometimes, he didn't like playing with the other kids, playing in groups, or playing with the "regular" boy toys. Instead, he took to numbers, letters, words, and math. Smart, funny, a natural animal lover, very creative and artistic, the other kids were very fond of him. We called him Mr. Popular all the time. My first. My beautiful boy.

Flash forward a few years, and at age eight we found out he was hearing impaired. I was devastated. What had I done? Why me? Why him? "Oh God" I thought to myself, how he must have been suffering. Well, children do say the darndest things and their perspectives are unencumbered, since they either have very small frames of references, or they really just don't see that the problem is as big as it can be made out to be.

Flash forward again a few years. After I had expressed to him how sorry I was that he has some challenges, and I wish he hadn't, he stated, "Mommy, it's ok...I can hear fine. I have these!" referring to his hearing aids. He then expressed that he's ok, and I should be ok, because he's ok, and that he doesn't feel any different. He said he feels lucky to have me as his mother. I was floored by how optimistic he was, and how mature to have the wherewithal to think and say such a grown-up thing. I was humbled and I felt, at that moment, like I was the lucky one.

Child number two, also gifted, is beautiful and comes with added value. She doesn't sleep well at night, or for long, and like her brother she prefers, sometimes, to play solo. She too is very artistic and creative, funny, and has always had her own food preferences. Now a pre-teen, and again like her brother, she loves her computer so the rules of the house have to be a bit strict to ensure they get outside to bike ride, rollerblade, or run around chasing each other to avoid a fight. Born with kindness about her, she is my animal-whisperer and has a connection with animals that is as caring as a mother to a child, like my son. Child #3, who is also gifted and born all grown-up, feeling left out by the fact that she's the smallest, shortest, and youngest.

All my children were born with a very strong sense of self, sense of justice, and a natural born instinct to contribute and make a difference. How lucky we are. But I still didn't get to pick, and the road of today has been spattered with some bumps, hurdles, and mountains. So what's the choice? Do we have one? Is there a choice when the going gets tough? Yes. For me, it was to try harder, keep going, and never give up. And things got really tough for a while there – each child had their issues like every family does.

Early on, I was a stay-at-home-mom while hubby worked twenty-three hours a day as a Patent Agent, building up his experience so one day he could open his own successful Patent and Trademark Firm. And that he did. Life was hectic, busy, emotional, lonely, challenging. There were some days I would call my husband on the phone begging him to come home and help. I was a basket-case. Even my split-ends were splitting ends. My world was topsy-turvy. How did this happen? My life felt like it was spinning out of control, and I'm your proverbial Type-A control freak. Can you imagine how that must have felt for me? It was all too much. What could I do? There was no help, and I pretty much kept to myself. No one really knew how I was feeling. I kept everyone out. I'd get up every day, put a smile on my face, and make the best of it. Three kids were a lot. They fought a lot. They each had their demands and needs that had to be met and I did my best. But it was wearing on me. My husband helped when and where he could, but it never seemed like it was enough. And then one day, it happened. I realized that my life was getting the better of me, and it was taking a toll on everyone. My kids, myself, my husband....and then it hit me. I realized that the one thing, the biggest thing that was getting in my way was myself. I was the elephant in the room. I had been trying to fit every square peg I could find into that round hole, forcing it to fit and it never did. I was my biggest enemy. I had been fighting for years what I thought were certain circumstances that were against me, and everything that happened to me was being done TO me. My ego was so inflated; it was disparaging everything and everyone. I wanted certain things about my life to change, and when it didn't, or wouldn't, I fought it. I was the common denominator in all this. And there I was, on the floor, with the realization of the century--if anything was going to change, it was me. I had to change. I had to be the change; shift my mindset and change my perspective. It was going to be the only way I could give to my children, husband, and myself.

It was at that moment, on the floor at 10 a.m. in workout clothes that I realized everything that had happened TO me up until then, happened FOR me. I suddenly realized my own self love is from the heart of gratitude. I was thankful. I was thankful for the fact that the universe picked ME to be the mother of my children because I was deemed to be the best for them. The right person. The chosen one. That all of my experiences were not just for my children, but also for me. To make me a better person, so I could help my husband be a better person, and to be the mother that my children need. Had I not experienced all that I had in my life with my husband and children, I would not have been able to become the person that I started becoming from that day forward. It was a gift. But not just to me, and for me, but for others, you, them, him, and her. I can't regret anything. I wish I hadn't felt so much inner struggle and angst, but what a gift I see it became. Picking myself up off the floor, I found myself staring at the mirror, full of love, happiness, validation and conviction. I Am Empowered. I am a woman, hear me roar. I am who I am because my kids need me. My husband needs me. I need me. I realized something even more pivotal at that moment too; that all my challenges, efforts, tribulations, and triumphs are for others. It was my calling. Not the lawyer I wanted to be since I was four, not just the mother I had become, not only the wife I was committed to being, but a source and resource for others to come to find help and support.

I got to choose. I changed my mindset, my manner, my mandate. I was no longer going to fight. I was already winning at the exact things I thought were crippling me. Today, my life is full of happiness and gratitude. I'm still learning, still working on perceptions, and still defining what makes life good and wonderful even when it feels like it isn't. Today, I get to help men and women, like yourself, realize what you've got ain't so bad. The grass isn't always greener on the other side. In fact, usually it isn't. The grass is only greener where you water it. Not my quote, but it works and it's true. The only authentic way we have of salvaging ourselves is to realize how wonderful we are with all that we give, share, and know. Throwing in the towel isn't an option. We all have value and gifts that are ours alone, that only we know how to work and give to others in a manner that they may help, heal, support, connect, and enrich. The basis of our humanity is connectedness and we each have so many wonderful gifts and offerings to share. Sometimes it takes a bit of darkness to shed light on what's most apparent, and when it does, look out, because the world becomes so much brighter.

I help men and women improve their relationships and communication so they can have happier, more fulfilling, connected, and peaceful lives. This is what I decided my purpose was going to be from that moment onward, from that moment I picked myself up off the floor. I knew right then and there that if I could help it, I was going to be there for whoever needed me so they wouldn't have to feel like they were hostage to emotional destitution and inner strife one second longer than they had to. And you don't have to. You're not alone with feeling struggle, fear, loneliness, or that black hole of sinking into the abyss fast with no way out, no one to save you, and no answers or solutions. There are answers. There are solutions and there are choices. Today, I live being and feeling thankful to my past, to my children, and to my struggles. They have all shaped me into the woman I am today. I get to wake up every day and arm my children with my best knowledge and my deepest love, knowing that I am special to them and that I was chosen for them. I get to wake up every day and help hundreds of men and women feel better about themselves, empower them, and teach them who to live the lives they really want and have the kind of relationships that are fulfilling, connected, and validating.

I've had many happy times in my life, but when the road was bumpy, I never gave myself a choice to change the way I saw things and interpreted them. I learned I do have a choice. I can control many of my outcomes, and can control how I think, what I think, and even when I think what I think. I have choices. You have choices. WE have choices. We can live loving ourselves with gratitude, from the bottom of our hearts every day. Today. Sprinkles and whipped cream, anyone?

YOU ARE EMPOWERED.

LOVE
FOR
THE GREATER
GOOD

~

OUR

OUTER CIRCLE

RELATIONSHIPS

ANITA SECHESKY

Anita is a Registered Nurse, Certified Life Coach, International Best Selling Author x 3, Speaker, Trainer, Publisher, NLP and LOA Wealth Practitioner, as well as Big Vision Consultant. She is the CEO and Owner of Anita Sechesky - Living Without Limitations. Anita has assisted many people break through their own limiting beliefs in life and business. She has two International Best Sellers and is launching her first solo book *"Absolutely YOU! –Overcome False Limitations and Reach Your Full Potential"* in November 2014. As a professional compiler and publisher, Anita can help you to put your passion on paper.

www.anitasechesky.com
asechesky@hotmail.ca

SEVENTEEN

....

LOVE FOR THE GREATER GOOD
OUR OUTER CIRCLE RELATIONSHIPS

When was the last time you actually realized you were someone else's outer circle relationship, meaning you had no emotional connections to this person, yet there they were doing something for you to help make your day or life better? Maybe you had gone through something serious or traumatic requiring assistance, or it could have been as simple as having car troubles and that person was the one who helped you out. You didn't refuse the assistance and it was thoroughly appreciated with gratitude.

My reason for including this as part of the third theme within this beautiful book compilation is that I realize we can never address love for others enough. Personally I believe that this is exactly what the whole concept of world peace is all about – reaching out to help others who may never be able to ever reciprocate it. We all have a role in how we choose to make a difference in the lives of those around us who are not part of our daily interactions.

For the most part, we just go about our daily lives not considering what's going on outside of our immediate outreach. Social media has made it seem that the world is in our backyard. When we hear the latest news of what's happening somewhere else, we both react and respond right away or we tune out of that particular event, avoiding further reports as it may overwhelm us outside of our comfort zone or our physical reach. In reality nothing can be further from the truth. Although we see via our computers, smart phones, television, and newspaper or hear on the airwaves, we are still disconnected in a dysfunctional sort of way. You see we are triggered to evoke emotional responses based on the fact that we are passionate beings with extensive personal connections we share life experiences and memories with. This explains why, when we hear of disconcerting things like natural disasters and disease outbreaks, we become concerned because of the fear of vulnerability and of how it may affect so many lives. As a result, there are many people who choose to step outside of their comfort zone and risk their own health and well-being or sacrifice their time to help make a difference in the lives of complete strangers. When a person begins to understand how valuable their small acts of kindness and generosity are for the greater good, and how the impact becomes immeasurable and so much more valuable, it becomes a heart-warming experience.

The co-authors in this section all share a common goal or vision which involves actively contributing their lives in some way to helping those outside of their close circle. They can see the greatness in all people and believe that everyone deserves a chance to create a better life for themselves. It is truly an honor to partner with people of such high caliber and integrity.

I believe we all contribute to the greater good – at times consciously unaware of it, by supporting for example a local organization that in turn sponsors an international humanitarian project. I'm sure that if we carefully examined our connections in life we would find so many individuals that dedicate themselves in some way to help make a difference in the world. I also believe that one must truly love themselves in order to purely love others without repression. One must have love in their heart for all of those closest to them, or else how could they honestly love those with whom they have no biological connection? The true reality in loving yourself requires you to let go of everything that does not serve your greatest self any longer. Choosing to love your inner circle connections or those who truly know and appreciate you sets your love apart. If you don't allow others to negatively influence you, you'll always attract love back into your life. You have made your love factor very focused and clear. You are Love! In a sense this increases the value that you see in yourself because you choose to not allow others to control your thoughts and opinions about your love for others.

When you consider the time it takes to manage our responsibilities and roles, think how much more of an added accountability it is for others to do so with a free mind and will. I believe it takes a person with a big heart to appreciate the life they have, all the relationships they've been blessed with, and even extend themselves to people who will never say "Thank you" or try to repay the kindness and generosity they have received.

This world if filled with people who possess so much potential, yet many feel that they cannot do anything with their lives. They no longer have dreams or desires because they are so discouraged and demoralized by life. This confirms why I believe there is so much remaining for us to do, whether in the smallest to the greatest of ways that we see possible. If we choose to help individuals, who are hopeless and without passion, make a better life for themselves and their loved ones then we have brought a little piece of heaven to earth. There are already many established organizations worldwide that can use the support and then there are things we can do right here in our neighborhoods: food drives for homeless shelters, volunteering on community organizations, and church groups engaging in community work are just but a few. The point is for us to get started if we have never done so before.

As a Registered Nurse, I have volunteered with fundraisers to help build financial assistance so that certain specific organizations can assist families who have lost their homes in a fire, for example. Plus these same partnerships also participate with international aide. Choose your associations wisely and if applicable, select one that is close to your heart.

I know that our world is filled with beautiful people. I have provided nursing care to people from various regions around the world. My experience has been very positive and I appreciate everyone. What an amazing world we have! We can learn so much from each other as we embrace our differences, bring our needs and goals together, and accept all individuals as equally valuable.

"Love without Borders"

When was the last time you allowed yourself to just fall in "LOVE?" Were you thinking very hard, or did it just happen like that?

Did you know before you stepped up to the plate? What was next? What's happening inside you? Was the feeling intense? Did you know it had to be real?

What made you stop and take a second look? Why were you so surprised when things just made sense?

Are you feeling Empowered? Enlightened? Encouraged? Elevated?

Does everything just come naturally? Was the connection unbelievable or are you still in denial? Are you still scared of what's happening deep inside?

Are you trying to reason with yourself? Are you still putting things into place or changing your perspective?

Was it sudden, or did it just develop in a way that you had no control? Do you still have butterflies? Will you take it for granted and allow anything to just happen or will you nature it and let it develop into what it is meant to be?

Do you have the patience to stand close and shower it with the love and attention it deserves?

How long are you willing to wait? Do you understand the intensity behind the words and emotions? Are you playing games, or are you mature enough to handle the Explosion of Passion that is building up deep inside?

"LOVE" can make you rich, break down barriers, destroy hate, change lives, reroute destinies, rebuild nations, empower the weak, enlighten, rebuild hope, open deaf ears, conquer fears , give vision, save humanity, control the wicked, ignite passions, stop wars, correct mistakes, heal the broken, save the lost, connect the pieces, restore the years and seal two lives for all Eternity!

Love IS the fountain of youth!

Are you ready to live a life full of "Love without Borders"?

Anita Sechesky

REBECCA DAVID

Rebecca is a certified Life & Health Coach, an International Best-Selling Author and a passionate entrepreneur! She has created a rewarding career path as a holistic life coach & entrepreneur. Her work is dedicated to empowering people love life and live in vibrant health. She engages in continuing education in the fields of functional nutrition & health, personal development and holistic remedies. She investigates the root cause of the issue rather than just treating symptoms. She is a woman of great faith, compassionate, inspiring and one who fully embraces the entrepreneurial journey! Rebecca was born in Southeast Michigan, USA, and currently resides there near her children and grandchildren.

rebecca@rebeccadavid.com
facebook.com/RebeccaDavidOnline

EIGHTEEN

....

CULTIVATING GRATITUDE

Thank you for joining me on this journey of Love, Gratitude & Hope! What a fabulous journey it is!! Do you agree? If you're hesitating to answer "Yes" then stick around. Hopefully you'll fully embrace this beautiful truth very soon.

First I want to express that I am truly grateful for this opportunity to write about a topic that has blessed my life enormously and continues to bless and transform my life daily. It is my hope to encourage you to begin cultivating gratitude today. As you do you'll begin to reap the rewards of a more joyful and peaceful life. It is amazing how something as simple as a change in your thinking or a shift in your perspective can often immediately result in a sense of relief or peacefulness that was not evident when the focus was on the difficulty.

Have you ever noticed how bad you felt when you experienced a difficult situation in your life and you began to focus on all the negative things about it? The more you rehearse it over and over in your mind or in your conversations the worse you began to feel. I've had that experience myself and know firsthand it is very uncomfortable and can drain the life right out of you!

Have you ever had the opposite experience of being in a difficult situation but instead of focusing on and speaking of the negative you shifted your thoughts or perspective to something positive and it resulted in lifting the despair you were feeling? I've experienced that as well and can honestly say this makes a huge difference, maybe not in the situation itself but certainly inwardly regarding the stress level, or lack of stress that you may be feeling. The difference in your attitude, thoughts, or your perspective can and will completely change the way you feel. This shift doesn't usually change the current challenging circumstances but it can change how you feel and allow you to be a much more peaceful person and bring tranquility to others as well.

Our lives are so full of many experiences that involve a variety of spectrums. There are seasons of trials & struggle and there are seasons of blessings and ease. We experience it all and we are not always privileged to know when the season is about to change and suddenly take us from one spectrum to another.

Here's something to consider: What if you had such a strong inner-peace that no matter the circumstance you were going through outwardly your inner life remained at rest? The inner-peace & joy I speak of is certainly possible for you. It is achieved through gratitude. Life's difficulties can be so hard at times but don't wait for them to change before you are able to have peace and joy. Make a decision today to begin to find things to be grateful for and acknowledge them. This will help ease the hard times. You'll see.

Gratitude is a choice and must be cultivated consistently in order to reap the full rewards. By cultivating gratitude you will begin to find the beauty and blessings in every situation. No matter the season, you will remain steady and equipped to handle it. Just as the farmer must cultivate the hard, dry land to turn it into fertile soil, we must continually cultivate an attitude of gratitude to reap its harvest. The farmer begins with dry, hard ground and tiny seeds in his hands. He knows the potential of those seeds and the greatness and abundance that can come out of them when properly cared for. He tills the land, plants the tiny seeds, and works consistently to nourish the soil so the seed will bring forth all the potential within it.

When you cultivate an attitude of gratitude you will be tilling the soil of your mind, heart, and spirit. The effort you put into cultivating and nourishing gratitude will multiply the occasions you have to be grateful. Like the tiny seed of potential, the cultivated gratitude within you will produce an abundant attitude that recognizes more and more to be grateful for. The frequent expressions of gratitude will nourish your life fully and sustain you throughout each season whether it is a season of struggle or ease. It's a beautiful practice to begin and end every day with gratitude. I encourage you to get yourself into this habit. Each and every day brings with it opportunity to express gratitude if you have a willingness to see all that you can be grateful for. The more you are aware of the little or big things to be grateful for, the more will become obvious in your life.

I've seen and felt the incredible vibrant energy that radiates from those who recognize the bountiful things to be grateful for in their life! It's an energy that lifts them higher above the mundane and discouragement that is prevalent in the world. Those who express gratitude daily stand out from the crowd. They have a magnetism that draws others to them. People want to be around those who have hope, those who are celebrating life, and those who are uplifting and encouraging. Those who regularly express gratitude are also healthier in their body, mind, and spirit.

Are you someone who has not yet embraced the gratitude life? Are you hurting inside and wondering when you'll be able to feel the love and life that you see expressed in others? Is it difficult for you to find something to be grateful for because your life is hard, you're having problems with your health, or you are overly concerned with the health of a loved one? There are many reasons or excuses that someone may not feel it's possible to live in gratitude but I can assure you that thankfulness can make those difficulties seem much more tolerable. It may seem like those who express appreciation frequently do not have much in their life to bring them down. It may look like their life is so much easier than yours or others who have hardships, but let me tell you that those who live a life of gratitude and love do experience many of the same hurts and struggles as those who are bitter and angry. A very big difference between the two types of people is their inner joy, the peace, and the beautiful hope that permeates from those who are able to find the beauty in spite of or in the middle of their struggle. Those who are quick to express appreciation are often the ones who have experienced some of the worst pain, yet they shine from within knowing the beauty and blessings that fill their life through the acknowledgement of gratitude along the way.

You have a choice when reflecting on something. You can chose to see it in a positive or negative view. Often things happen in our lives or the life of a loved one that is so devastating we cannot see something to be grateful for within that situation. In these difficult times, it's important to take time to quiet your mind, breathe deeply and look for at least one thing to be thankful about. When this is practiced over and over, you will begin to automatically see something in every situation that you are able to express gratitude over. Difficult situations are an opportunity to learn & grow. There is so much outside of our control but feeling and expressing thankfulness is a choice available to all of us all the time. The rewards are well worth it and will change your life for the better.

It's great to see many expressions of appreciation on social media lately. Have you joined in and taken a gratitude challenge? It used to be common to only see this during the Thanksgiving season, but I am pleased to say I have seen it more frequently the last couple of years. Those who are participating are reaping the rewards indeed. They are living a more joyful life and are able to bounce back quickly when trials come their way. Perhaps I am seeing a lot of it because of the people I choose to be associated with. I encourage you to surround yourself with those who have a heart of thankfulness and express it often.

Journaling is a great way to exercise your gratitude muscle, if you haven't begun a journal yet I encourage you to do so now. Here is a beautiful tip to enhance your journaling experience and cultivate a deeper awareness of appreciation: When you write down something you are thankful for, take the time to express the reason why. I've been practicing this for a long time but when I took it to the next level of expressing 'why', it brought my experience to a much richer and more meaningful place. I encourage you to practice this as well. You'll be satisfied you did. You may continue to take each expression of appreciation to a deeper level by conveying even more reasons you feel thankful. Perhaps consider what your day or your life would be like without it and then be sure to fully embrace your acknowledgement. This is truly cultivating gratefulness!

Our thoughts create our reality and nothing was created without thinking of it first. If you desire more in your life to be grateful for then begin to cultivate a grateful attitude. Express yourself verbally or through writing of the little things that may seem so obvious to you and then state why you are thankful for it. This practice will begin to open up a new awareness and appreciation within you. Create a habit of doing this before bed and you'll rest peacefully. Choose this habit to begin the day and you'll be sure to invite more positive things into each day.

I believe in God as my creator and I believe in His word the Bible as my instruction manual to live the life He created me to live. His word says there is life and power in the tongue. The spoken word can bless or curse your life. I acknowledge my gifts of love that came from my heart of thankfulness. God has blessed me and I am so appreciative I have eyes to see & ears to hear it! I have cultivated this love until it became an automatic response in my life. You can do the same if you choose. Set a daily intention for yourself to begin nurturing thanks. Be a gratitude ambassador and express yourself daily!

I am excited to be a co-author in this book of love and hope; an anthology written by a collection of beautiful souls who give you a little glimpse into their lives through one of their personal stories.

In my previous publications *"Living Without Limitations – 30 Mentors to Rock Your World"* as well as in *"Living Without Limitations – 30 Stories to Heal your World"*, I have enlightened readers about using their gifts and talents. I have also shared about overcoming my health issue of Fibromyalgia. It is a great privilege to be part of this book and offer words of encouragement to you.

My passion is healthy living and to be supportive to those who desire to live their best life possible. I am grateful to work in a profession where I coach others to be their best self: physically, spiritually, mentally, and emotionally. I love to connect with people, encourage them to look past their current circumstances, and find hope to live the life they desire – one of health, gratitude, faith, and purpose.

MONICA KUNZEKWEGUTA

Monica is a Certified Life Coach, CEO at Dream to Action Life Coaching, International Best Selling Author, Mastermind Facilitator and project Founder of Inspiration for Kids International. Passionate about life coaching, she believes that real wealth is hidden in everyone. After obtaining her Degree in Sociology in 1993 she moved to the United Kingdom. Her experience managing Mental Health projects and working in the Care sector in general spans over a period of 20 years. Her organization Inspiration for Kids International donates library books to children in rural Zimbabwe and allows Monica to be part of a movement that nurtures the imaginations and education of children.

www.dreamtoactionlifecoaching.com
mkkunze@yahoo.co.uk

NINETEEN

....

INSPIRING OTHERS TO SHINE

am a Zimbabwean woman. I am educated. This is not as nearly as commonplace or as simple as you might think. This is my story and yet, it is not merely my own. It is the story of countless girls and boys, of communities, of countries, our world, and the hopes we all have to be able to follow our dreams.

I completed my primary education in the rural areas of Zimbabwe. I belonged to a community that did not promote or support the education of its girls. This was my early introduction into the plight of disadvantaged children, lacking exposure to books, information, solid education, and a world ripe with opportunity. Even though Zimbabwe has the highest literacy rate in Africa at around 97%, it isn't always easy to come by especially for the children in poor communities.

Despite these early challenges, I managed to complete my 'O' levels (something equivalent to high school) within that environment. My best friend was not so lucky. At the age of thirteen, she was told she could no longer attend school although her parents could have afforded to send her to any school in the land.

Thirteen at the time as well, I was devastated for her. No schooling? I couldn't believe it. I quickly became determined to help her. I even gathered information on long distance learning to share with her. Sadly, she died from an illness before I had the chance to see her again.

Looking back, I realize now that I had not considered the logistics of my plan at all – the tuition, postage, study time, or how she would have concealed her studies from her parents and the close relatives who were also against the idea of educating a girl child. In my desperation to empower her with this chance, all I had been able to think about were possibilities.

Possibilities; her story haunted my life. Eventually, her story and my need to try to help her formed the seed of my passion to help other children receive educational opportunities and became part of the purpose that drives me.

In 2007, through a Leadership and self-Expression program, I was challenged to design and execute a twelve week community service project aimed at giving back to my own community. This was to be done without expecting anything in return. The project itself was supposed to be so big that it scared you. Mine was and it did. Fuelled by passion, I knew I wanted to impact the education of the youth by providing books and materials to the schools but I had no idea how to make it happen.

Still, I began compiling books and through word of mouth, it began to take shape. I met a teacher who talked to a friend from another school. As it happens, their school was about to get rid of thousands of books. I contacted libraries; I had no idea they replace books after every five years. I was simply amazed at how the opportunities, resources, donations, and people flowed together to make it all possible. In no time I had thousands of books, pens, pencils, and even toys. These were donated to an orphanage.

Twelve weeks later, my project and my passion had become a reality. Inspiration for Kids International was born. I had collected more than three thousand books in the U.K, shipped them to Zimbabwe, and arrived to personally deliver them to the schools. A dream that began in my mind and heart years and years before had finally come true.

But there was more to come. The day before one of the deliveries, I had decided to take a walk to the school to prepare them for the upcoming donation. Along my way, I met with ten children who were playing outside a grocery store located about 200 meters from the school grounds. Since it was during the regular school hours, I inquired about why they were not in school and was told that they had all been sent home to collect their school fees or tuition fees.

After purchasing a soft drink for myself, I began asking further questions of the children. It turned out that the arrears varied from one term's fee to the tuition cost for an entire year. The kids also told me they were afraid to go home because they felt that their parents would not do anything about the fees as this was not the first time this had happened. They had simply planned to wait for the end of day and return home as though they had attended a normal school day.

As the discussion continued, I was shocked to discover that the amount I had spent on a drink was all that was needed to pay for their education for the whole term. The idea hit me right in the pit of my stomach and I felt physically sick at the thought. I kept thinking, "Thirty cents. Thirty cents is all that stands between a child and education?" It weighed so heavily on my heart that I didn't even want the drink anymore.

Slowly, shock and disbelief gave way to new determination and a new idea began to grow. I had come here to impact education by bringing books. This was so much bigger than that and yet, I could help them far more than I'd even imagined when I'd first arrived.

I asked the children if they wanted to go back to school. Seven of them agreed to go with me to the head Teacher's office while three chose to go home. We walked back to the school and I was filled with excitement and blessing at the possibility presented to me here. Once there, I paid for all their fees for the year. It wasn't much for me, but it wasn't about the money at all. It was about the issue of education and giving children every opportunity to grow, to dream, and to reach their full potential.

The following day, I returned to present the books. It was deeply personal for me, even more so now than when I'd first had this dream. I was extremely blessed that my father was able to join me to see a first-hand example of how his support for my education has allowed me to help support others.

While there, I was able to personally encourage the children to pursue their education, expand their imaginations, and follow their own dreams. I made sure to give a special message of hope and encouragement to the girls because I still feel they need more support in these challenging times where so often it seems many are being denied education and basic human rights instead of being nurtured, empowered, and supported to be their fullest, best selves. My heart is drawn to bring them hope when and where I can.

I am humbled every time I receive a beautiful letter from those who share with me how they've been inspired to follow a certain career or life path because of the books and information they now have available to them. I am presently preparing the next book donation through Inspiration for Kids International and continue to for look ways to do even more.

Once, as I was sharing some of my experiences, someone said to me, "You've had a very difficult life!" At one time, I would probably have simply agreed with them and saw nearly every aspect of my life as a challenge, often a painful one at that. I reflect back to the days when my continued education was frowned upon. Escaping childhood marriage, physical abuse from peers, and the heartache from torment of jealous for those close to me – it was often a difficult road but as I ponder this now, I am convinced that each of these experiences worked together to prepare me for this moment, right here and right now. I realize that it was all necessary to help me master the principles required to live a fulfilled life and to live in harmony. Those experiences have also provided me with my own unique way to give back to my community and to the world.

Had I not fought to go to school and witnessed the disadvantages on such a deeply personal level, I would not be so moved by the plight of the millions of children who continue to be affected by this. I would not possess the passion or compassion for others, especially the youth, or for education that spurs me to do what I can to change this. Children and women remain at the centre of my purpose.

Despite the initial resistance within my village, other families began sending their own daughters to continue their educations after witnessing how my education allowed me additional ways and means to help support my family and reach out to my community. The very community which did not encourage sending girls to school has now built its own primary and secondary school with more children being educated. I feel proud that my father is one of the people overseeing the building and construction of this school.

Through my experiences I have discovered my life's purpose, which is to inspire and guide women and children to reach their fullest potential and achieve their dreams. It is with inner determination and self-motivation that I desire to see them prosper and flourish. When one of us 'wins', we all win.

Look around you and look at your own life. Look at what you've gone through. Consider lessons you have gained from your experiences. Notice the ways in which you have developed certain aptitudes, passions, or sensitivities, and how in some cases may have even carved out a direction or career based on those things.

Some of your most difficult experiences were part of preparing you for your purpose, and for this moment. Step into the light, it is time for each of us to step up. Your ability to inspire others cannot be taken for granted. Neither can your ability to help transform your world. Once you've embraced your life as it is right now, not as you would have liked it to be, you can more clearly see ways to contribute to creating a better world for yourself and for others.

If you want to bring about a change, start with one action today. What one thing can you do right now? Want to make a difference in your own community? Look at the things that speak to your own passion and experience. Do you have a heart for animals, for the environment, for the elderly, for children, for the disabled? You can have more than one project and all of them serving one goal – fulfilling your purpose. Do not wait for someone else to begin. Start the ball rolling. Share your ideas, thoughts, hopes, and aspirations. Find the right team or people who want to build you up, encourage you, and help you to grow. Find yourself a coach or join a mastermind group. Take charge of your life and leave a legacy. Very famous people have belonged to mastermind groups. Mastermind is now being described as the staple tool for successful individuals. We live in an era where technology is making it possible for us to find resources and information. The world is now borderless – do not lag behind. There is nothing wrong with leaving those who want to hold us back.

You have got something of value to give. Never underestimate your power and your ability to recreate your life. We all have our own paths and our unique way of giving or serving. Allow your authentic nature to shine. Don't be surprised when God makes a way for you to fulfil your purpose and serve the greater good beyond your wildest dreams.

EUGEMA INGS

Eugema was born and raised in southern Ontario. She is a wife, mother, entrepreneur, Registered Early Childhood Educator, and is a Certified member of AECEO (Association of Early Childhood Educators Ontario). She has been a front line worker, instructor at community colleges, sat on various advocacy groups, and was elected as a council member for the College of Early Childhood Educators of Ontario. Eugema continues to volunteer, organize and participate in local events within her broader community. She currently resides in a small Northern community Murillo, Ontario, and enjoys camping in the summer and cross country skiing and snowmobiling in her trails in the winter.

eugemaings@yahoo.ca
facebook.com/GemaOnt

TWENTY

....

A HEART TO VOLUNTEER

You want me to do what?! The big word is "volunteering". The first thing going through my mind is: Do I have time? Do I really want to do this? What will my kids or husband say? What will I get out of it? Is it really worth doing or is it more of a gossip club?

These are questions that arise when we are asked to volunteer. Being a professional, I did not have the opportunity to be part of my children's class volunteering as I would have loved to participate. Back then, mothers or fathers would come and get involved with their child's class. My husband volunteered for my daughter's kindergarten class when they went skating. He would take an early lunch so he could spend time with our daughter on the ice (as well as help with other children's skates). Talk about father daughter bonding!

First let's look at volunteering. There are so many ways we can give our time. Our children's school, community groups, within our own professions, church groups, families or friends. An individual can be either in the forefront or behind the scenes. I love volunteering. The question is: Why do I do it? The simple answer is that I enjoy it. One of the volunteer groups has a recognition certificate which takes a few years to complete. The idea is to write out what you have volunteered for and what you contributed and learned. I was quite surprised how much volunteering has helped me. It has improved my personality, enabled me to meet new people across Canada and abroad, boosted my self-esteem, and improved my time management and communication skills.

As a teenager, I loved singing and playing the guitar. I was asked to lead the praise and worship for our youth group. I was quite excited and agreed. The youth group consisted of young people whom I knew. I was already an organizer and leader plus it was something I enjoyed doing. Because of the location of our church in relation to where the youth resided, we were unable to practice. It all seemed to work out whenever we got together. I believed we went over the songs prior to the start of our meetings. Everyone involved was committed and had quite a bit of fun. Being in this position helped me improve my guitar playing, singing, and organization skills.

I recall our youth leader asking for a few volunteers to prepare a message on anything we were interested in. Now I was always interested in Angels, and this gave me an opportunity to learn more. Well, that week, I did quite a bit of research (back then there was no internet) using books. The following week, not only was I excited to share what I learned, but I was curious to find out from the youth if they ever heard of some of these angels. I gave a verbal presentation but also drew pictures to explain the various angels. I will never forget that presentation: it was quite a learning experience not only for me but for the other youth.

As I progressed into young adulthood (even though I had changed churches), I continued involving myself with praise and worship with the youth group. What did I receive from volunteering? Research skills, presenting in front of people, and abilities to share my non-artistic abilities!

When I became married, I moved to a small town in Northern Ontario. We started attending a local church. My husband and I, being younger members of the congregation, were asked to lead children's church as well as the youth group. We did this for a few years. Not only did we learn from the children, teens, and lessons we taught, we formed a basis of trust with all involved. I never knew this until we told the youth that we were resigning from our positions as we were starting a family of our own. It was then that I realized how some of the youth who were especially troubled relied on us. I stated that our door was always open to them; they could come over to talk or just have us listen. We would be there for them. We missed the youth as the majority of them resided in the community and did not come to regular services.

I continued playing guitar and singing in the main praise and worship band. We would practice throughout the week learning new songs, tweaking other songs, and ensuring we were prepared for Sunday's service. At the end of our practice sessions, we would have fun just jamming and singing. I felt I was giving back to the lady who had originally taught me as a young teen to play guitar with the agreement I would play in their church band. Unfortunately my family had moved so I was unable to fulfill the agreement on my part in that community – now I could fulfill it in spirit.

I loved going to concerts, especially weekend ones. To give you a bit of a background, my first weekend Christian music festival was in 1985. My parents dropped my brothers and I off on a Friday. They helped set up our tents and said, "See you Sunday." I had a blast! That started me wanting to go to concerts. This brings me to another endeavor. I was asked by an individual who was running a local spot on TV showing Christian bands. Knowing that my husband and I were up to date at the time with the Christian band scene, he asked if I could host the show. This was new for me. Wanting a challenge, I talked it over with my husband and I went for it. I was nervous even though I had cue cards. After a while, I became comfortable and was able to speak from the heart introducing bands I had personally met or had seen in concert. I did this on top of everything else for close to a year. When my daughter was born, it became a bit difficult having her in the hearing room while I was recording so I gave it up even though I enjoyed it.

On a professional level residing in a small town, it was hard to receive any training within my field. I had the opportunity to get involved with a group that did advocacy work for my profession. I volunteered to be the go-to person for my jurisdiction. Aside from petitioning the public (which was a real eye opener) I had the opportunity to set up meetings with MPs (provincial politicians). I was totally excited about having a debate. I pictured a great deliberation with all the different candidates discussing child care. I was disappointed when only a few nominees responded stating that they were unable to make it, disgusted when others did not even acknowledge the invitation but excited when one came out. Instead of a debate, it turned into an interview. It went quite well. I learned that politics was a whole new ball game. It was a real learning experience!

As my children entered a new school, I had the opportunity to volunteer in their classroom for a few months. When I started working full time, I was unable to volunteer during the day, however I wanted to know what was going on. My daughter's teacher had asked me if I wanted to sit on the parent council. Not really knowing what it was about, I agreed and showed up at meetings. I felt really uncomfortable not knowing anyone in the room aside from the principal. The group was very professional and they were used to working with each other. As I had come in three months prior to the end of the school year I was totally clueless. I sat, watched and listened. By the autumn, we had moved so my children went to a new school. I made sure I went to the Parent Council and Home and School Association meetings. These groups held their meetings one after another so it took time to learn what was really happening. Both groups had different guidelines and policies they followed. I enjoyed both groups knowing that, as a parent, I could have a voice in what we could do to improve, enhance and aid all students learning experience within the school. During those years, I not only volunteered to sit on these committees but had responsibilities. I became secretary for both groups. I took minutes for both meetings, typed the minutes out on my home computer, and emailed them to the chair of one group and president of the other group. I enjoyed this position and remained in it for quite a few years.

When we had our Annual Meeting for our area, no one was volunteering. Everyone was told that if no one filled the spots the group would shut down. I was so used to having organizations around that I never thought of one shutting down owing to a lack of volunteers. I spoke up and stated I would sit as Vice President providing someone would fill the Presidents spot plus having the old Executive willing to support the new executive. Fortunately people stood up and we came out with an Executive for our region. Was I scared for speaking up? Not scared but nervous. I had no idea what they did at that level. After reading previous minutes, asking questions, and looking at the website, I finally got an idea of what I was getting into. I went from Vice President to President in a short period of time. It was a learning curve on which I welcomed the help and advice of others who were volunteers within the organization.

Now as my children have grown into young adults, I look back and review what I have contributed to society. Did I make a difference within my church, community and profession? In my church, I hope the children and youth went away with a firm layer added to their foundation in life. I hope the people who participated in praise and worship were able to incorporate songs of inspiration and worship within their daily lives. In the community, workshops were provided to parents and youth. Within my profession, I continue to advocate as well as sit on a self- regulatory council. This has contributed to positive changes within my field and government.

Breaking my volunteering into three categories, did I personally get anything out of it? Aside from what I already stated, I improved in public speaking and writing resolutions, enhanced my listening skills, acquired the ability to read people, learned more about government policies and regulations, learned how to advocate, became a self-regulator, better note taker and report writer, became proficient at planning events which included tasks from flying speakers in to putting together agendas for the day, and writing proposals. I am sure there are quite a few other things I could mention that I am continuing to improve on my journey.

How did my family react to my volunteering over the years? My kids accepted it as part of everyday life since I had been volunteering prior to their birth. My husband was on board most of the time. If I had meetings more than once a week, I knew it was cutting into my family time. I knew it frustrated my husband if I had quite a few meetings during a week. As for my children, when I showed up at their school, that would embarrass them. Who wants their mom at school? Picking up or dropping off something (kids would do it once in a while if it kept mom out of the building) at school during the day was difficult to co-ordinate with my full time job, but I worked it out. Time management!

Volunteering does affect everyone! You can be proud of who you are and what you are contributing to society. If you want to change, enhance or learn something, you need to get involved doing something you enjoy! Not sure? Take a deep breath, a leap of faith, and take action! Give it a try!

BARBARA A. SCOTT

Barbara is a Strategic Business and Technology Executive, Management Consultant, Social Media Content Marketer, Life Coach, Speaker, Writer, Mother of three young adults and grandmother to one grandson and one granddaughter. Leveraging her years of experience in the business and technology arenas she combines her passion for people, process and technology and her skills as a Six Sigma black belt in process engineering, to design, develop and assist businesses with the implementation of the process frameworks necessary for delivering consistent quality results and coaches individuals on how to easily apply these scientific principles in their daily life to continuously improve the quality of their lives.

coach@myvideocoach.com
barbara.alice.scott@facebook.com

TWENTY-ONE

....

I BELIEVE IN YOU

M y parents allowed my brother and I the opportunity to choose our religion. Don't get me wrong, they believed in a higher power they called God but both had grown up in religions that were forced upon them through family tradition and culture or as prescribed by the practice of each particular religious philosophy or belief. My mother told me that we were all children of God and taught me that one should "Do unto others as you would have them do unto you." That being the case, as I grew up I had the opportunity to explore, with my extended family and friends, the teachings of many different religious congregations including Baptists, Catholics, Methodists, Jehovah's Witnesses, Mormons, and the list goes on. The underlying principles of all those religions seemed to be based on the concept of love and faith in a higher power.

What I discovered for myself was that there is only One Truth, but many paths that lead you there. Just as Jesus wasn't a Christian and Buddha wasn't a Buddhist, I subscribe to no religion. I am a spiritual being living a human experience in the physical form here on earth. A being that has been given labels since conception.

Even before each of us are born in this earthly form, the ways we find to separate ourselves from one another begins, not only in terms of religion but in terms of gender, race, social class, and geography. This discernment is purely based on conditioning and beliefs of each individual being. No two of us ever truly understand the same One Truth in the same way. The truth is, 'that's okay'.

The important thing is for each of us to live our truth. If we say we love one another, treat those you meet as your brother. Don't judge others unless you yourself are free of reasons to be judged, and live that truth. The planet would be a much more peaceful place to live. Growing up with my mother who was a natural born caregiver, I learned to have compassion for the needs of others and saw how beautiful it was to be in the service of others making their lives better just because of her presence. She taught me so many things without trying but just by living her truth. She was, is, and always will be my light.

No Race

In school when I would have to fill out those forms where you select your gender, age, and race I always selected "other". My brother and I were neither white nor black nor Hispanic; we were "other." Our father was a Caucasian male and our mother was a Hispanic female. In the 1960s that was still considered an interracial marriage highly frowned upon by the white community. As a result my father did not allow my mother to speak Spanish to us as children so we never learned her native language. Over time, she lost much of her own ability to speak the language herself.

I learned what it felt like to be judged for the color of my skin as my mother had been. Even though I was half Caucasian, white children didn't see me as one of them and because I could not speak their language, Hispanic children didn't see me as one of them either. Being excluded provided me the opportunity to have compassion for others who were also excluded for whatever the reason. The underdogs, the black sheep, and the 'weirdos of society were all just like me. They cried when they were sad, they laughed when they were happy, and they bled when they were cut. They too must have felt hurt when they were excluded, just like me.

I first understood the pain of exclusion as a little girl watching a classic animated television show. I saw how all of the other reindeer wouldn't play reindeer games with him because he had a red nose. He was different, just like me. It made me weep.

I eventually learned that I was not only different because of the color of my skin and the "hand-me-down" clothes I wore, but also because of the size of my parent's bank account. Poverty kept me from being a cheerleader, from playing an instrument, or from any other school activity in which participation cost money. I realized that poverty is also a label that separates and excludes human beings from the right to basic needs such as shelter, clothing, and food. Despite growing up with very little, my mother always told me that I could be anything I wanted to be when I grew up. I believed her and she believed in me. I didn't know how, but I knew that the 'poverty label' was not for me and I vowed to break free.

No Place

The year was 1975 and I was ten years old. Pulling up into a driveway my sleepy eyed cloudy awareness quickly transformed into a keen sense of awe as we had finally arrived to the incredible desert paradise I had dreamed about. Our old truck which carried a camper on its back, like a hump on a camel's back, represented the only home we had along with the contents inside, our only belongings. This was not the first time we moved, nor would it be the last. From grade one to grade six, I attended thirteen different elementary schools. Most people assumed the reason was that we were a military family but it wasn't. My mother was committed to our family and always followed my father and his elusive dreams. At the time I wished that we didn't move so much. Having to make new friends and start over in school was never easy, but that experience gave me the courage that I possess today to travel alone across the nation and to other countries around the world.

Dr. T was the principal at the elementary school I attended the year we lived in the desert. He was bound to a wheelchair from an accident. He was different and that somehow allowed him to see that I was different too. He gave me opportunities that I had never experienced before. I was on the safety patrol, a cafeteria helper, a playground monitor, and he would take me out of class to give me what I now know were knowledge, skills, IQ tests, and to play backgammon with him. That year I somehow understood that being different was my key to freedom from poverty. He managed to keep track of me through all the years and all the moves until he passed away last year. I had the opportunity to thank him years later when I finally understood how much he had meant to my personal growth and success. He made me feel special, not different. I believed him and he believed in me, until I learned to believe in myself.

No Limits

After discovering when I believed in myself, as my mother and Dr. T did, there truly were no limits to the possibilities for my life. My success has fueled my desire to give back. I wanted to find someone else to believe in, until they could believe in themselves. As a consultant, speaker, and coach earning six-figures, I travel frequently. It's varied, unpredictable, and doesn't allow for much continuity. That makes it difficult to commit to locally based volunteer programs. Being the technology geek that I am, I knew there must be a way to volunteer and give back through the use of technology – and thankfully I was right. I became a video mentor to a boy in South Africa over four years ago. After the first year of mentoring, I wanted to meet him in person because I felt that I could be a better mentor if I understood his situation, how he lived, and what his true challenges were by actually seeing them first hand. It was during that trip that I realized the need was very great there. So many human beings were being excluded by the color of their skin and the label of poverty; the kind of poverty and living conditions that make it hard to believe in anything, including yourself, or the possibility for a better life.

My heart broke when I heard the stories of the children who lived at the orphanage. Many never knew their fathers, and lost their mothers to HIV or AIDS related illnesses. Yet, they were the lucky ones. They too had mentors that were helping them believe in themselves and the possibilities for their lives. At the orphanage they were provided meals and access to education; basic needs from which many of those living in the informal settlements and rural areas are excluded.

After my first trip I almost immediately began planning my return trip the following year but instead of going to work at an orphanage as I did on the first project, I decided to go on my own as a 'total immersion' volunteer. Living in the community would provide me the opportunity to truly understand the daily lives of those individuals who are struggling to believe in a better future for themselves. I discovered that the generation of learners matriculating and graduating from college are among the first "born frees" – or those born after Apartheid. Many of their parents forfeited their education in order to insure that their children would have a right to one. Now they are unable to make a living wage, so their children are suffering the consequences: inadequate housing, lack of adequate nutrition, and an education system that is struggling to keep up with the rest of the world. I had to find a way to provide support for more than just my mentee and the other children I had taken under my wing. I wasn't sure how, but I knew I wanted to give back in a bigger way.

I returned to South Africa this year once again. Now, using the knowledge, skills, and experience I have accumulated in my two decades of building consultative relationships, managing full lifecycle projects, and executing strategies to grow, improve, and innovate businesses, I designed a concept for a community based, multi-purpose, self-funding technology center to empower people through education, internship, and employment opportunities that will enable them to move from poverty to property. I found many supporters for the concept and am hopeful that once realized my vision for Wizdom SA will not only create jobs, but a sense of community while weaving a support system that believes in everyone's dreams.

No government, corporation, or organization alone can solve the economic, societal, or environmental challenges that exist today. It's going to take the people. One person at a time, we can change the world.

As a Change Agent, I spend many hours volunteering my time and experience mentoring and coaching the future leaders in some of the most impoverished communities in South Africa. Until funding comes through for my project, I am 'believing in' those young leaders in those shack communities called informal settlements, while they too learn to believe in themselves. This generation of young adults realizes that they can no longer continue to wait for the government to solve the problems that exist in their communities. They are working together and taking action to find solutions to problems that have existed for the last two decades. With just a little encouragement and support they are accomplishing great things. If they continue to believe in unlimited possibilities there are no limits to what they will achieve.

You too can make a difference in the lives of others. Find someone to believe in, and believe in them until they can learn to believe in themselves. It will change your world. It will change their world. I know it changed mine.

JEY JEYAKANTHAN

Jey is a highly successful entrepreneur and I.T. professional with over 22 years' experience in Business Development, Project Management, & Business Transformation for Fortune-200 companies. In 2011, Jey founded AVAJ Future Solutions. AVAJ is a Toronto-based company specializing in the creation of Mobile Apps Development and Web Design. Jey is actively involved with many volunteer and advocacy organizations in Canada and currently holds the position of Director for the Sophia Hilton Foundation of Canada and was also a member of Markham Board of Trade & Canadian Tamils' Chamber of Commerce.

www.avaj.ca
jey@avaj.ca

TWENTY-TWO

....

A NEW REALITY

Growing up in the small village of Kokuvil, Jaffna, in the country of Sri Lanka, I was not privileged to believe in success. From this part of the world, success meant to survive another day. Our small village was part of a war-torn climate that did not have any guarantees of living through the week. My life was filled with the overwhelming knowledge of the fact that at any given time, we would have to run for our lives and seek shelter in the bunkers which were underground and a normal part of our house structure. We never knew when an attack would strike our village.

It was bittersweet time of growing into the young man I became. I cannot put into words what it felt like to live a life where you had no ambitions or goals in life because you never knew if you had a future to look forward to. For me personally, this was something that was truer than many realize about my life. I had gone through the loss of some of the closest people to me, and who were a significant part of my life. My best friend was a young man whose only hope of inspiration in life was to become part of the rebel group that attacked my hometown village. He joined forces with the very thing that took his life and future away. At the tender age of 13, not too long after becoming a rebel fighter, he was killed. I also lost people who were not blood-related but were close as family.

Thankfully my family immigrated to Canada when I was in my late teens. It was a whole new world. My thoughts were totally on a different level than your regular teenager. Organized sports, clubs, and yearbooks were not on my agenda. I was discovering what it was like to be living in a country without that constant need for survival. I began to understanding that it was alright to let my guard down and not worry about new friends coming back and attacking my house. I learned that borrowing books from a library and bringing them home was perfectly acceptable. It was normal to own more than a few outfits. It was okay to finally be me.

I entered High School as an older student. I may have been older, a lot wiser, and seen things that no one should have ever seen, but I realized I had an opportunity for a free education which I was going to take full advantage. I completed my high school education and then continued onward first to College and then to University. This is where I met my beautiful wife and life started to take on a whole new hope and direction. I discovered how much potential I had to strive for all of sudden.

My life is exactly how I want it to be now. I have achieved goals that I never thought were even possible when I was growing up. I have dreams to fulfill that life is giving me. I grew up in a family-oriented lifestyle where values are very strong and close. I have so much to be grateful for now. When I think of the things that I never had myself growing up, I am overjoyed to be able to give my children them, just like any father would.

As a parent, I have gone through the stress of having a child who was diagnosed with a condition and then had surgery at a very well know children's hospital. I experienced the process of having my daughter receive the care and support to help her recover and heal from her sensitive operation needed for survival. It was truly a miracle to witness this happen and I am so grateful. Because of this experience, my wife and I have become very involved in helping to support and fundraise for that hospital through my company.

My business is always doing things within the community. Right now it is at a small scale, but I plan on being involved within community service in a much bigger way. My heart goes out towards people who have uprooted their lives from their home country and come to Canada so they can make a better home for their families. As my company expands, I want to give back to this community. It does not matter to me which country people are coming from, we have all experienced the transition of change and are developing a life of expectations and dreams. Right now, I am engaging my business with helping organizations involved in human rights as well as medical research. My company also sponsors my daughter's school and since funding is tight at times, we donate tablets. As a volunteer of the school council, my family brings in school instruments to help the children.

I enjoy helping my staff attend motivational speaking and self-development training. As an Immigrant, I strongly want to empower my staff. They can gain credibility by working for our company to gain hours, training, and expertise skills through apprenticeship programs. These programs will enable them to pursue higher paying jobs when they have completed the required hours and training. My company will endorse and recommend them as valuable contributors to the IT Profession upon completion. Being a number one mobile App specialist in Toronto, this is a valuable asset for them to begin a new and successful career in Canada.

I am drawn to positive and authentic people who are ambitious and are doing something for the greater good. I enjoy meeting new people and learning more about others. There was a time in my life I grew up in an environment where I didn't know positivity and success. It was not something that was around me and it was never talked about. My family basically lived day to day just hoping we would all be together by the next morning and if we were, that was good enough. We never had motivational materials, television, or books to empower and encourage us to dream of a life without impossibilities. I am so grateful for the opportunities life has given and continues to give. I believe the Universe is a sincere thing that will give you what you put out there. I always see the good in others and as a business-minded individual I can see so many unlimited possibilities. My experience in business has brought me very far and the dream is still going strong. I am a very happy person now. If you see a guy smiling, who is kind of quiet and just plain happy, wave your hand and say, "Hi. I would love to get to know you."

There is so much to learn from each other when you are open to just being a nice person. Even though my focus is not on wealth and money, my company is doing well. We are considered the top Internet Technology Company in Toronto for building Mobile Apps and web design. You can imagine we work with very elite clientele but at the same time, I enjoy helping the small business owner take their operation to the next level by utilizing our highly skilled staff. My life is filled with so many amazing moments. I am actively involved with my community in which I can see so much potential and am excited to bring my motivation and knowledge to help empower those who did not have the inspirations as myself at one time in life. We can all make a better life if we choose to look at the positive things and believe more in ourselves. I came from a place where there was no hope for a future of any kind of accomplishment. Just thinking that I can do it inspires me to want to do more. I am grateful that my children will live a life without fear and worry about their loved ones and friends as I did growing up. There is so much to be happy and appreciative of in this life when we look around us, why complain? I love education and have enjoyed pursuing my career. When I moved to this new country as a teenager, I had a choice to make. Was I going to just be average and do what was required or was I going to give it all I have? I chose to do the best and strove to become the best at everything I did. I have received numerous prestigious awards from institutes of learning and I believe a good education is one of the keys as well as having an open mind to understand people and things in life. My father gave his family everything he could and this is what I try to do in my life, with my family, and my business. I consider my business as family. I care about the best interest of my employees.

JEREMY ROGERS

Jeremy was born in Mesa, Arizona. He moved to the Seattle area at the age of sixteen and has been there ever since. He has worked as an auto-mechanic for the majority of his life. Though he finds fulfillment reviving broken down cars, his real passion is helping people. He desires to make a big impact in the world by assisting others in healing their emotional scars. Jeremy seeks out those who are often overlooked by others and brings joy into their lives by building them up and making them feel important. He believes everyone has special gifts and abilities that makes us all equal.

jeremydr33@gmail.com
facebook.com/jeremy.rogers.167527?fref=ts

TWENTY-THREE

....

REACHING OUT TO OTHERS

So many people in the world see others differently from themselves. Perhaps those other persons are physically or mentally handicapped, maybe they don't wear the same clothing or drive the same car, or they don't have the same viewpoints or religious beliefs. People shun them, turn away from them in their time of need, or worse, treat them with callousness. How sad it is when someone views themselves as being above another person. How awful it is when one person finds the need to be cruel to another. What they don't realize is that these acts are just as harmful to themselves as they are to the other person. My hope in writing this story is to bring more awareness of the damage that is brought upon the world when we are unkind to others so that each person who reads this message can take a look within themselves and find more compassion for those around them, no matter who they are or where they come from. If you will do that, I assure you that your life will be richly blessed.

People with disabilities tend to be prime targets for ridicule because they usually can't defend themselves. Children who have emotional insecurities are also likely to be candidates for bullying. As a child, I was one of those kids who was made fun of and bullied because I was different. Learning in school was a struggle for me and I took longer than most kids to understand and process the concepts my teacher taught, so my parents made the decision to hold me back after kindergarten and I ended up taking that grade twice. Going to school every day for the next several years and watching my classmates always one year ahead of me was uncomfortable as it was a constant reminder that I wasn't good enough to pass something as simple as kindergarten. As I watched my classmates move on to first grade, leaving me behind, I felt dumb and worthless. The more my self-esteem suffered, the more difficulty I had with learning and I became convinced there was something wrong with me. The teacher I had in my second year of kindergarten had little patience for me because I didn't comprehend the material as quickly as she expected. She perpetually became irritated with me, slamming books down on my desk out of frustration. I felt like a HUGE failure. To make matters worse, I had poor eyesight and wore these hideous glasses that had tape on them because they were broken and my parents couldn't afford to buy me a new pair. I looked like the classic "nerd" and was called such by the other students; my self-esteem worsened with each passing day.

I didn't have many friends when I was young, but there were two older boys from church that befriended me and made me feel important. They treated me with respect and always took the time to talk with me. Around them, I was able to smile, laugh, and be myself. I felt comfortable with them because they didn't judge me and their friendship seemed genuine. It didn't matter to them what I wore or how well I did in school. These two young men made a lasting impact on my life and I made the decision to be like them and help others feel as good as I felt when these two boys were near.

I sought out friendships with other children who were considered outcasts. It was my desire to be the kind of person that made others feel good and let them know they were important despite what others thought. I wanted to make a difference in their lives the way my friends had done for me. I had compassion for others because I knew what it was like to feel the loneliness of not having friends to hang out with during school recess. I found my friendships with these children to be very rewarding. I saw the smiles of excitement on their faces from the simple fact that I was paying attention to them while others pretended they didn't exist. The delight they expressed around me gave me a feeling that I too was important. They knew immediately that I accepted them for who they were and they also accepted me for who I was. It didn't matter to them that I wasn't the most popular kid in school. Although I was far from "Mr. Cool" to the other I kids, I was cool in THEIR eyes. I knew how to make them laugh; I knew how to help them forget about their struggles; I knew how to make them feel like somebody. It was through my friendships with these children that I realized I had a gift for helping people open up, look past their hindrances or disabilities, and feel better about themselves. I learned that I was blessed with an ability to help others recognize their strengths and talents when they didn't believe they had any.

As I developed more and more friendships with those who were less fortunate than me, my self-esteem began to improve. I felt fulfilled when I was able to assist another person with their problems and it allowed me to forget about my own challenges. I found strengths in myself that I never knew I had. I realized my opinions were important. Through my compassion for others, I learned that it was alright that I didn't do as well in school as many of my peers. I gained a better understanding of who I was and what my purpose in life was. I began to see my self-worth.

Throughout my life, I have continued to seek out others in need and have found constant satisfaction in easing another person's burdens. When I was eighteen, I became friends with a boy a couple of years younger than me who had been born with a spinal condition which caused him to have difficulty walking. I had bought him a set of crutches to aid him with getting around. He was ecstatic when he realized it was a lot easier to walk with the crutches – like having a new set of legs – and soon he was practically running! That friendship has blessed both him and me. I fixed cars for a living and he was very skilled with mechanical work. We worked well as a team because he knew how to do things I didn't know. He became my right-hand-man. As we worked together, I was able to help him supplement his income and he was able to help me stay in business. He was trustworthy with cars as well as money. We still have a close friendship to this day and I know I can rely on him when I need assistance.

Another good friend I have is an older gentleman with a mental handicap. When I met him, he was living in a hotel receiving disability income from the state, but the money was not given directly to him. The money went to a cousin of his who was in charge of dispersing the money to pay his expenses. Unfortunately, his cousin was dishonest and not using the money to pay the expenses. My friend was kicked out of the hotel and stuck living on the streets with little to no food, so I would take him out to eat or buy him groceries. Some friends and I rallied together and we were eventually able to get him out of his situation. We found a new place for him to live and we got the state to allocate a new person to manage his money so his expenses were paid consistently. My friendship with this man brought joy to my life. We both had a passion for singing and would hang out together and perform karaoke. We would also go to the cheap movie theater together. Before the movie would start we would visit the arcade room and play a zombie killing game. Although I've never been a fan of video games, I had a lot of fun playing this particular game with him because he would light up with excitement. Being with him made me feel good. Although he was older than me, his disability made him childlike and I felt like I was bringing my "son" to the movies. Every time he asked, "Are we going to buy popcorn? Can we get some candy? Are we getting drinks?" He found pleasure in simple things and I felt wonderful for being able to make his day special through little acts of kindness.

I have a friendship with an older lady in her eighties. She was divorced many years ago and never remarried. I sensed a loneliness about her so I took to her like she was my grandmother. She calls me when she needs something done around her house. Sometimes I think she finds things for me to do just so I will come over and visit. When I leave her house, I never depart empty handed as she is always sure to send me away with my hands full of cookies or pies. She occasionally forgets how long she has them sitting around her house and, because of her poor eyesight, doesn't notice the mold growing on them. Nonetheless, I always take what she gives me (even if I don't eat it) because I know my acceptance of her gift means the world to her.

Most people just don't take the time to talk to others like the amazing people whom I have developed memorable friendships with. Sadly, individuals don't take the time to get to know and understand who my friends are and the remarkable qualities they possess. Though they have little, they would give you all they had. I just couldn't imagine hurting or ridiculing someone like that.

The problem with the world today is that too many people focus on themselves. They are constantly thinking, "What can I do to get ahead?" They focus on their own problems and hurry too much to solve the troubles in their own lives. What they don't realize is that if they took the time to slow down and think of others, they would be able to free up space in their mind to work through their challenges. If they would look around themselves and stop to help someone else in need, they would find their trials are not as bad as they seem because there is someone with bigger struggles. As they seek to ease another's burdens, they will feel their own burdens lighten because when they help others, help will come back around to them.

You don't need to knock someone else down to get ahead. When you reach out to others, that's how you get ahead because you will feel better about yourself, your self-esteem will improve, and you will feel positive about who you are and where you are headed.

We are all in this world together. We all want to feel important and accepted. I can only imagine how much more amazing this world would be if people realized how easy it is to lift another person up. All it takes is a simple word of kindness or encouragement, a smile, or a listening ear to make a difference in somebody's life. When you take a few minutes to get to know someone and understand who they are, you can greatly bless their life, and your life in turn will be enriched.

I challenge you to take a look at how you treat human beings. Be sure to have compassion for others and I promise you will notice an amazing transformation within yourself. When you do something to lift another's soul, your soul will also be lifted.

Offering kindness to people is like playing a game of dominoes. When you reach out with understanding and compassion toward another individual, you will make a difference in their life. You will make someone feel like they matter and help them feel better about themselves and they will in turn stretch forth their hand with compassion to other people, and so on, and the kindness will spread. Through you, this world can become a better place.

KEITH MILNE

Keith is an insightful leader involved in non-governmental not for profit fields in healthcare, social services, and other people caring businesses. Leadership and organizational development are key interests. Keith has served communities as a counselor, minister, manager of a shelter for homeless people as well as serving on community boards and committees. As an effective public speaker he provides insight and motivation for individual change, overcoming challenges, and organizational development. With a keen interest in people, Keith is developing a business model of consultation that focuses on the need of individuals and organizations for an effective, compassionate, in depth listener, that leads to a successful interaction.

keithdmilne@hotmail.ca

TWENTY-FOUR

....

SMALL LOVE EQUALS BIG IMPACT

Recently I went to visit a friend who I hadn't seen for several years. Often when we see friends from the past, there is the possibility of apprehension or nervousness, thinking about the reality that we have both traveled separate journeys, have aged, and sometimes even illness has visited. My friend had suffered a stroke a few years earlier, so I was wondering how that had affected him. Any worries I had quickly evaporated as I stepped into his home and was greeted with a giant bear hug, a beaming smile, and "I have missed you my brother!" The atmosphere of love led to a wonderful time of visiting and recalling so much of the past, both pleasurable and painful, and the future possibilities of our journeys.

Our friendship began in some difficult times. I was serving our small community as a part-time chaplain at the local hospital when one of the doctors asked if I would talk with his patient who, while detoxing, was waiting for a spot to open up in a treatment program. I'm not an expert in the struggles of addiction, in fact I'm quite naive, but I work within the context of love for people. I practice attentive listening motivated by the choice of love.

For twenty odd years our paths had crossed, mingled, mangled, and somehow progressed to a very deep friendship. My friend's journey had taken him through many circumstances and over many distances. From that humble point in time, he attended college for retraining, became involved in the field of social work, effectively working with the homeless and street population. He became an expert in street health and outreach, becoming involved at a national and international level with significant impact in shaping the methodology people utilized around the world. It all began with a simple conversation within that context of listening with love.

Love is the multifaceted term that contains strong connotations. It means treating people with respect, looking for the best interest of others, and it is the best motivation for doing good. I do believe that however you may interact with people, if the real motivation from your perspective is love, then the effect will be positive. I do not mean we have to wander around our lives with the warm fuzzies, but living our lives with a commitment to speak and act for the best interest of our fellow beings. This also means not looking for our own rewards. Love does not say "What's in it for me?"

Severe mental illness is a disturbing disproportionate part of life with many homeless people. I worked in a shelter for homeless people for several years and witnessed both the suffering and the occasional miracle. An outreach worker from the psychiatric hospital asked us for a referral of a person that we felt would be a great challenge. We all said the same name and so began his engagement process. We watched with interest as this worker slowly and patiently engaged the person of interest. I cannot recall one time in the previous two or three years when this client had ever spoken one coherent sentence. It was always a challenge to encourage him to shower or follow any personal hygiene routine. Yet, persistently the worker would arrive two or three times a week to engage the client, eventually going for coffee or going for a walk. After several months of gaining trust the worker suggested he would like to move the client to another shelter to provide easier access to the hospital and hopefully a more stable environment. We often saw this worker as he came in to work with other clients and he would report that the first person was doing okay!

A couple years had passed when the worker came in with a second person and with a twinkle in his eyes he asked the staff to call me downstairs from my office. I was intrigued to be introduced to this clean-cut warm individual whom I did not recognize until he spoke. Then I was simply amazed. For about twenty minutes we conversed, as he told me about his new apartment in a specialized supportive housing unit, living with a roommate, taking part in community activities and living a full engaging life. I was in awe as I witnessed this magnificent change and with tears welling up thanked that worker for his patience and love with which he practiced his occupation.

Sometimes it is the little things that we say or do that begins the steps of building people and communities. Simply one step at a time or sometimes one smile at a time. Often it is taking the time to carefully listen to a person as they talk about their journey, their difficult challenges, or the crisis they are currently experiencing.

Recently a friend was trying to describe a person he thought I would know. His description was, "I met this guy at the hospital. He's always smiling and he greets everyone. He has this twinkle in his eyes and makes you feel like you are the center of his attention." With laughter I recognized the description of a chaplain that I have known for years and have seen in action. The positive impact this chaplain has shared with people over the years is truly immeasurable. Attentive and purposeful listening is the beginning of a loving commitment to walk with you through your time of crisis and need. When we find role models whom we can emulate, we need to learn, and then follow that example.

After over twenty years of leadership, management, and practice in the people caring business I made a radical change of direction to end up behind the wheel of a transport truck. What began as a somewhat romantic adventure quickly faced the reality that there is a lot of hard work involved in this occupation. However, I have also realized that this attitude of love for people is needed in the workplace. Many times I have found myself in the parking lot, the yard, and the docks or while driving, listening to people vent their frustrations. Even while driving, truckers communicate with each other on the radio or through various signals to other truckers. Usually that communication is from a positive perspective as we help each other get to our destinations safely. Unfortunately there are times when we experience negativism, particularly as people express anger, frustrations, and racism. One sunny day I was driving through my favorite National Park, where the speed limits are reduced due to the amount of wild animals that often calmly walk across the highway or gather as a group to lick the pavement and stop traffic. As another truck approached I could see a driver who is part of a visible minority that I know experience aggressive racism within the industry. When our trucks came closer I gave this driver a big friendly wave and a smile. At first he was startled, and then I saw a big smile and knew that at least for a few more miles that driver would be encouraged.

The rewards of living your life with a deep commitment of love are sometimes immediate, but most often long term or not even discernible. True love is not about the rewards for us but is really a commitment of a way to live. Love really does transcend all boundaries and you will make a positive difference where you are, whether in the workplace, the community, or far beyond.

We can talk about it. We can dream of doing great things. Without real action it (love) is nothing. So it is with a mindful commitment that we begin to take action in our lives. Our aim needs to be consistency with our actions without hesitancy. Don't wait for better circumstances, for a better environment – don't wait for anything, just start taking action. Choose your action, wherever you find yourself and make love a way of life, a lifestyle of activities – but you must start.

Here are three of the finest examples of people I believe who have loved their world – Gandhi, King Jr. and Mandela. They are truly examples who have changed history and moved the mountains of prejudice and hatred with love. However, each one would have failed if their love had just been of words without action. Gandhi would have failed if he had not made that long trek to the ocean to make salt.

King's voice would have been silenced except that he got out from behind the pulpit, led the march, and stood firm in the face of physical threat. Mandela refused to hate and become bitter, and instead donned a football jersey. Each leader loved with action and therefore achieved success.

An old man was asked, "Why do you get up early in the morning every day to pick up garbage and sweep the sidewalks and gutters of our street?" His reply was simple "I love my neighbors. I love my world!"

You CAN do something.

CONCLUSION

My intention with this project was to inspire each and every reader to re-evaluate their lives and how they have allowed past experiences to affect themselves. With the various personal perspectives explained in this book relating to one of the three themes, it would be a blessing to see how my book can influence healing the world with love, peace, and unity. I encourage each of you to stretch and let go of your own personal limitations my dear readers as you continue to ponder the wisdom and experiences of these co-authors. They have openly allowed you into their world of emotions and experiences.

Now that you have read my Anthology project, it is my hope that you can see how each of these inspirational chapters have contributed to make my vision for this book come to life. I trust that you will feel a healing shift in your own world. Love is a powerful remedy for many things that ail mankind.

The value that is within this book is priceless. Just like gold never loses its value, the knowledge these contributors poured into their chapters is incalculable and worthy of review and application in one's daily life.

Now, my question to you is "Do you have a book inside of you waiting to be written and published?" I can help you to compile, organize, and get your book out there. Working with me and my professional team as I mentor you on this journey will give you so much confidence to create your own powerful masterpiece. You are a visionary with so much potential inside of you. What are you waiting for?

I have successfully managed, mentored, consulted, and organized three groups of international best-selling co-authors in less than one year. That's approximately 75 people from around the world who are recognized as leaders and experts among their peers! Now as a publisher, I want to assist you every step of the way to create your own Best Seller!

I would love to help you to organize and manage your book project, or even create your business from the ground up, centered around your vision/theme of your own anthology project.

This is what I enjoy most about empowering individuals or groups of people so they can reach their goals in as short of time possible and then see their productive results! I have learned through experience and my extensive training as a Level 3 – Advanced Certified Life Coach, NLP Practitioner, Law of Attraction Wealth Practitioner and Registered Nurse how people cope effectively by having an organized system that brings balance with positive results! There really is a secret to helping others succeed just for you! I want to show you how to live your life with passion and purpose.

It's not always easy to keep things running smoothly, whether it relates to a company, your business, or managing a group of people, while building the life of your dreams. I understand the frustrations, tears, and stress. I want to assist you making your dreams and goals a reality.

Together we can develop a "Master Plan for your own success" and along the way eliminate any "Limiting Beliefs" that have been stopping you all this time. You may even be surprised at what you discover! Your passion is where your strength is. My passion is all about bringing your passion to life.

Let's get your book started! Connect with me and let me mentor and coach you on how you can step into "Living your Life without Limitations!"

asechesky@hotmail.ca
With much Love and Appreciation,
Anita Sechesky